Last Days of the Buddha

Last Days of the Buddha

THE MAHĀPARINIBBĀNA SUTTA

Translated from the Pāli by
Sister Vajirā & Francis Story

Revised Edition

Buddhist Publication Society
Kandy • Sri Lanka

Buddhist Publication Society
P.O. Box 61
54, Sangharaja Mawatha
Kandy, Sri Lanka

1st edition	1964
Reprinted	1974
Revised edition	1988
2nd revised edition	1998

ISBN 955–9219–98–7

Printed in Sri Lanka by
Karunaratne & Sons Ltd.
647, Kularatne Mawatha
Colombo 10

Contents

Foreword

The translation of the Mahāparinibbāna Sutta which is offered here is a work of collaboration, but is based upon a text prepared by Sister Vajirā of Germany, to whom credit for the initial work must be given. The final revision of the text was done by Mr Francis Story. The notes and references which, it is hoped, will help in the understanding of the text have been contributed by the Venerable Nyanaponika Mahāthera, much of the material for them being taken from the Pāli Commentary.

Every effort has been made to give a faithful rendering of the original Pāli. The greater part of the sutta is straightforward narrative, but it also includes references to profound aspects of the Dhamma, which have to be understood in their precise meaning if the full import of the Buddha's last exhortations is to be conveyed. In the choice which inevitably arises between terminological exactitude and literary form, the translators have endeavoured to preserve the former with as little sacrifice as possible of the latter. Those who understand the difficulties of Pāli translation will appreciate that this is no easy task, and will readily overlook the absence of those literary graces which only a freer rendering would have permitted.

As in previous translations, some repetitions have been omitted and some repetitive passages condensed.

BUDDHIST PUBLICATION SOCIETY

Foreword to the Revised Edition

In this revised edition of *Last Days of the Buddha*, a number of stylistic changes have been made, aimed at improved readability. The word "Bhagavā," untranslated in the original edition, has been replaced by "the Blessed One"; several archaic expressions, which gave a slightly Biblical flavour to the diction, have been replaced by their modern counterparts; awkward sentences have been reformulated; and greater consistency was aimed at in the rendering of certain terms and expressions. The notes have also been revised in certain respects. The titles of the chapters and sections have been supplied by the translator and editors, though the division of the work into six recitation units dates back to the period when the Canon was transmitted orally from one generation to the next.

Introduction

Of the thirty-four discourses (suttas) that make up the Dīgha Nikāya (Collection of Long Discourses), ours, the sixteenth, is the longest, and so altogether maintains the first place where length is concerned.

It preserves the principal feature of the Buddhist sutta, insofar as it is, like others, a rehearsal of events as they have been witnessed. On account of its unique composition, however, it is, more than other suttas, capable not only of winning the affection of the pious Buddhist, as it naturally does, but also of attracting the general reader, since it is indeed a fine specimen of sacred universal literature.

It gives a good general idea of the Buddha's Teaching, too, even though it hardly offers anything that is not found—and often more extensively dealt with—in other suttas.

At the end of his life, after almost half a century's ministry, the Master had long since taught all that was necessary for attaining the ideal. During the last period his primary concern, therefore, was to impress on his followers the necessity of unflinchingly putting into practice those very same teachings: an appeal that could, of course, hardly fail in stirring their hearts more than ever before.

The Sangha came, indeed, to witness the greatest event in its history, and was keenly aware of it, especially since the Master had announced his Parinibbāna three months ahead. The impression on the bhikkhus who flocked to him in large numbers as he was pressing northward was tremendous, and could not fail to be reflected vividly in the oral account. (The

Buddhist canon was originally, as is well known, altogether oral.) Because of its particular import and abundance, this material was soon formed into one body; and so our sutta came to be.

In this connection, it is hardly possible not to remember gratefully the Venerable Ānanda. His share in the preservation of the Master's word is paramount to any other bhikkhu's, and his figure is inseparable from our texts. This was to become manifest for all time in the Mahāparinibbāna Sutta, which is plainly unimaginable without him. For it is Ānanda, and again Ānanda, whom the Master addresses, having tested for twenty-five years his sure grasp and brilliant memory and also his indefatigable personal devotion. But Ānanda too, here more than elsewhere, by his constant queries, worries, and amazements, becomes without intending it a central figure beside the Master himself, which undoubtedly increases the attractiveness of the text. Thus, then, Ānanda, gentle and pleasant as his name, and yet almost throughout his career incurring the reproach of the brethren, was immortalized along with his beloved Master, and—as we may add—along with his strange position between praise and blame, assuming mystic character in the third chapter.

The third chapter, almost exclusively, is devoted to depicting the circumstances connected with the Master's relinquishment of life, which is the dramatic culmination of events. It overwhelmingly drives home the purely metaphysical significance of the Parinibbāna, or at least ought to do so. For the Buddha neither succumbed to his fatal illness nor did he give way to the appeal of Māra (which is identical with the non-appeal of Ānanda), but sovereignly let go of existence at a timely hour, just as forty-five years earlier, on becoming fully enlightened, he had duly taken upon himself the wearisome task of teaching men. This fact is most thought-provoking, and consistently leads to the conclusion that by his Parinibbāna, indeed, the Buddha bore the last and highest possible testimony to his Teaching, which permits of no lingering inclination to self-preservation and continuance, but on the contrary reaches the highest exultation ending it all. The Master's Parinibbāna is, therefore, the one sorrowful event in the history of Buddhism that turns out, in its true meaning, to be really the most blissful.

SISTER VAJIRĀ

Ceylon
May 1961

The Mahāparinibbāna Sutta

Suppose, Ānanda, the river Ganges had become full to the brim, ford and all, drinkable for crows, and a weak man approached, thinking: "By the strength of my arms, I shall cut across and reach safely beyond!"—but he would not be able to do so. Even so, Ānanda, he who rejoices not when the dissolution of personality is being proclaimed, who is not pleased with it, who does not settle dwon in it and feels not released, such a one is comparable to that weak man.

Majjhima Nikāya No. 64

Homage to the Blessed One, the Holy One,
the Fully Enlightened One

Part One
In Magadha

1. Thus have I heard. Once the Blessed One[1] dwelt at Rājagaha, on the hill called Vultures' Peak. At that time the king of Magadha, Ajātasattu, son of the Videhi queen,[2] desired to wage war against the Vajjis. He spoke in this fashion: "These Vajjis, powerful and glorious as they are, I shall annihilate them, I shall make them perish, I shall utterly destroy them."

2. And Ajātasattu, the king of Magadha, addressed his chief minister, the brahmin Vassakāra, saying: "Come, brahmin, go to the Blessed One, pay homage in my name at his feet, wish him good health, strength, ease, vigour, and comfort, and speak thus: 'O Lord, Ajātasattu, the king of Magadha, desires to wage war against the Vajjis. He has spoken in this fashion: "These Vajjis, powerful and glorious as they are, I shall annihilate them, I shall make them perish, I shall utterly destroy them." ' And whatever the Blessed One should answer you, keep it well in mind and inform me; for Tathāgatas[3] do not speak falsely."

3. "Very well, sire," said the brahmin Vassakāra in assent to Ajātasattu, king of Magadha. And he ordered a large number of magnificent carriages to be made ready, mounted one himself, and accompanied by the rest, drove out to Rājagaha towards Vultures' Peak. He went by carriage as far

as the carriage could go, then dismounting, he approached the Blessed One on foot. After exchanging courteous greetings with the Blessed One, together with many pleasant words, he sat down at one side and addressed the Blessed One thus: "Venerable Gotama, Ajātasattu, the king of Magadha, pays homage at the feet of the Venerable Gotama and wishes him good health, strength, ease, vigour, and comfort. He desires to wage war against the Vajjis, and he has spoken in this fashion: 'These Vajjis, powerful and glorious as they are, I shall annihilate them, I shall make them perish, I shall utterly destroy them.' "

Conditions of a Nation's Welfare

4. At that time the Venerable Ānanda[4] was standing behind the Blessed One, fanning him, and the Blessed One addressed the Venerable Ānanda thus: "What have you heard, Ānanda: do the Vajjis have frequent gatherings, and are their meetings well attended?"

"I have heard, Lord, that this is so."

"So long, Ānanda, as this is the case, the growth of the Vajjis is to be expected, not their decline.

"What have you heard, Ānanda: do the Vajjis assemble and disperse peacefully and attend to their affairs in concord?"

"I have heard, Lord, that they do."

"So long, Ānanda, as this is the case, the growth of the Vajjis is to be expected, not their decline.

"What have you heard, Ānanda: do the Vajjis neither enact new decrees nor abolish existing ones, but proceed in accordance with their ancient constitutions?"

"I have heard, Lord, that they do."

"So long, Ānanda, as this is the case, the growth of the

Vajjis is to be expected, not their decline.

"What have you heard, Ānanda: do the Vajjis show respect, honour, esteem, and veneration towards their elders and think it worthwhile to listen to them?"

"I have heard, Lord, that they do."

"So long, Ānanda, as this is the case, the growth of the Vajjis is to be expected, not their decline.

"What have you heard, Ānanda: do the Vajjis refrain from abducting women and maidens of good families and from detaining them?"

"I have heard, Lord, that they refrain from doing so."

"So long, Ānanda, as this is the case, the growth of the Vajjis is to be expected, not their decline.

"What have you heard, Ānanda: do the Vajjis show respect, honour, esteem, and veneration towards their shrines, both those within the city and those outside it, and do not deprive them of the due offerings as given and made to them formerly?"

"I have heard, Lord, that they do venerate their shrines, and that they do not deprive them of their offerings."

"So long, Ānanda, as this is the case, the growth of the Vajjis is to be expected, not their decline.

"What have you heard, Ānanda: do the Vajjis duly protect and guard the arahats, so that those who have not come to the realm yet might do so, and those who have already come might live there in peace?"

"I have heard, Lord, that they do."

"So long, Ānanda, as this is the case, the growth of the Vajjis is to be expected, not their decline."

5. And the Blessed One addressed the brahmin Vassakāra in these words: "Once, brahmin, I dwelt at Vesālī, at the Sarandada shrine, and there it was that I taught the Vajjis

these seven conditions leading to (a nation's) welfare.[5] So long, brahmin, as these endure among the Vajjis, and the Vajjis are known for it, their growth is to be expected, not their decline."

Thereupon the brahmin Vassakāra spoke thus to the Blessed One: "If the Vajjis, Venerable Gotama, were endowed with only one or another of these conditions leading to welfare, their growth would have to be expected, not their decline. What then of all the seven? No harm, indeed, can be done to the Vajjis in battle by Magadha's king, Ajātasattu, except through treachery or discord. Well, then, Venerable Gotama, we will take our leave, for we have much to perform, much work to do."

"Do as now seems fit to you, brahmin." And the brahmin Vassakāra, the chief minister of Magadha, approving of the Blessed One's words and delighted by them, rose from his seat and departed.

Welfare of the Bhikkhus

6. Then, soon after Vassakāra's departure, the Blessed One addressed the Venerable Ānanda thus: "Go now, Ānanda, and assemble in the hall of audience as many bhikkhus as live around Rājagaha."

"Very well, Lord." And the Venerable Ānanda did as he was requested and informed the Blessed One: "The community of bhikkhus is assembled, Lord. Now let the Blessed One do as he wishes."

Thereupon the Blessed One rose from his seat, went up to the hall of audience, took his appointed seat there, and addressed the bhikkhus thus: "Seven conditions leading to welfare I shall set forth, bhikkhus. Listen and pay heed to what I shall say."

"So be it, Lord."

"The growth of the bhikkhus is to be expected, not their decline, bhikkhus, so long as they assemble frequently and in large numbers; meet and disperse peacefully and attend to the affairs of the Sangha in concord; so long as they appoint no new rules, and do not abolish the existing ones, but proceed in accordance with the code of training (Vinaya) laid down; so long as they show respect, honour, esteem, and veneration towards the elder bhikkhus, those of long standing, long gone forth, the fathers and leaders of the Sangha, and think it worthwhile to listen to them; so long as they do not come under the power of the craving that leads to fresh becoming; so long as they cherish the forest depths for their dwellings; so long as they establish themselves in mindfulness, so that virtuous brethren of the Order who have not come yet might do so, and those already come might live in peace; so long, bhikkhus, as these seven conditions leading to welfare endure among the bhikkhus and the bhikkhus are known for it, their growth is to be expected, not their decline.

7. "Seven further conditions leading to welfare I shall set forth, bhikkhus. Listen and pay heed to what I shall say."

"So be it, Lord."

"The growth of the bhikkhus is to be expected, not their decline, bhikkhus, so long as they do not delight in, are not pleased with, and are not fond of activities, talk, sleep, and company; so long as they do not harbour, do not come under the spell of evil desires; have no bad friends, associates, or companions; and so long as they do not stop halfway on account of some trifling achievement. So long, bhikkhus, as these seven conditions leading to welfare endure among the bhikkhus and the bhikkhus are known for it, their growth is to be expected, not their decline.

Seven Good Qualities[6]

8. "Seven further conditions leading to welfare I shall set forth, bhikkhus. Listen and pay heed to what I shall say."

"So be it, Lord."

"The growth of the bhikkhus is to be expected, not their decline, bhikkhus, so long as they shall have faith, so long as they have moral shame and fear of misconduct, are proficient in learning, resolute, mindful, and wise. So long, bhikkhus, as these seven conditions leading to welfare endure among the bhikkhus, and the bhikkhus are known for it, their growth is to be expected, not their decline.

Seven Factors of Enlightenment[7]

9. "Seven further conditions leading to welfare I shall set forth, bhikkhus. Listen and pay heed to what I shall say."

"So be it, Lord."

"The growth of the bhikkhus is to be expected, not their decline, bhikkhus, so long as they cultivate the seven factors of enlightenment, that is: mindfulness, investigation into phenomena, energy, bliss, tranquillity, concentration, and equanimity. So long, bhikkhus, as these seven conditions leading to welfare endure among the bhikkhus, and the bhikkhus are known for it, their growth is to be expected, not their decline.

Seven Perceptions

10. "Seven further conditions leading to welfare I shall set forth, bhikkhus. Listen and pay heed to what I shall say."

"So be it, Lord."

"The growth of the bhikkhus is to be expected, not their decline, bhikkhus, so long as they cultivate the perception of impermanence, of egolessness, of (the body's) impurity, of (the body's) wretchedness, of relinquishment, of dispassion, and of cessation. So long, bhikkhus, as these seven conditions leading to welfare endure among the bhikkhus, and the bhikkhus are known for it, their growth is to be expected, not their decline.

Six Conditions to be Remembered[8]

11. "Six further conditions leading to welfare I shall set forth, bhikkhus. Listen and pay heed to what I shall say."

"So be it, Lord."

"The growth of the bhikkhus is to be expected, not their decline, bhikkhus, so long as they attend on each other with loving-kindness in deed, word, and thought, both openly and in private; so long as in respect of what they receive as due offerings, even the contents of their alms bowls, they do not make use of them without sharing them with virtuous members of the community; so long as, in company with their brethren, they train themselves, openly and in private, in the rules of conduct, which are complete and perfect, spotless and pure, liberating, praised by the wise, uninfluenced (by mundane concerns), and favourable to concentration of mind; and in company with their brethren, preserve, openly and in private, the insight that is noble and liberating, and leads one who acts upon it to the utter destruction of suffering. So long, bhikkhus, as these six conditions leading to welfare endure among the bhikkhus, and the bhikkhus are known for it, their growth is to be expected, not their decline.

Counsel to the Bhikkhus

12. And the Blessed One, living at Rājagaha, at the hill called Vultures' Peak, often gave counsel to the bhikkhus

thus:

"Such and such is virtue; such and such is concentration; and such and such is wisdom.[9] Great becomes the fruit, great is the gain of concentration when it is fully developed by virtuous conduct; great becomes the fruit, great is the gain of wisdom when it is fully developed by concentration; utterly freed from the taints[10] of lust, becoming, and ignorance is the mind that is fully developed in wisdom."

13. When the Blessed One had stayed at Rājagaha as long as he pleased, he addressed the Venerable Ānanda thus: "Come, Ānanda, let us go to Ambalaṭṭhikā."

"So be it, Lord."

And the Blessed One took up his abode at Ambalaṭṭhikā, together with a large community of bhikkhus.

14. At Ambalaṭṭhikā the Blessed One came to stay in the king's rest house; and there, too, the Blessed One often gave counsel to the bhikkhus thus:

"Such and such is virtue; such and such is concentration; and such and such is wisdom. Great becomes the fruit, great is the gain of concentration when it is fully developed by virtuous conduct; great becomes the fruit, great is the gain of wisdom when it is fully developed by concentration; utterly freed from the taints of lust, becoming, and ignorance is the mind that is fully developed in wisdom."

15. When the Blessed One had stayed at Ambalaṭṭhikā as long as he pleased, he addressed the Venerable Ānanda thus: "Come, Ānanda, let us go to Nālandā."

"So be it, Lord."

And the Blessed One took up his abode at Nālandā together with a large community of bhikkhus, and came to stay in the mango grove of Pāvārika.

Sāriputta's Lion's Roar[11]

16. Then the Venerable Sāriputta went to the Blessed One, respectfully greeted him, sat down at one side, and spoke thus to him:

"This faith, Lord, I have in the Blessed One, that there has not been, there will not be, nor is there now, another recluse or brahmin more exalted in Enlightenment than the Blessed One."

"Lofty indeed is this speech of yours, Sāriputta, and lordly! A bold utterance, a veritable sounding of the lion's roar! But how is this, Sāriputta? Those Arahats, Fully Enlightened Ones of the past—do you have direct personal knowledge of all those Blessed Ones, as to their virtue, their meditation,[12] their wisdom, their abiding, and their emancipation?"[13]

"Not so, Lord."

"Then how is this, Sāriputta? Those Arahats, Fully Enlightened Ones of the future—do you have direct personal knowledge of all those Blessed Ones, as to their virtue, their meditation, their wisdom, their abiding, and their emancipation?"

"Not so, Lord."

"Then how is this, Sāriputta? Of me, who am at present the Arahat, the Fully Enlightened One, do you have direct personal knowledge as to my virtue, my meditation, my wisdom, my abiding, and my emancipation?"

"Not so, Lord."

"Then it is clear, Sāriputta, that you have no such direct personal knowledge of the Arahats, the Fully Enlightened Ones of the past, the future, and the present. How then dare you set forth a speech so lofty and lordly, an utterance so bold, a veritable sounding of the lion's roar, saying: 'This faith, Lord, I have in the Blessed One, that there has not been, there will not be, nor is there now another recluse or brahmin more exalted in Enlightenment than the Blessed One'?"

17. "No such direct personal knowledge, indeed, is mine, Lord, of the Arahats, the Fully Enlightened Ones of the past, the future, and the present; and yet I have come to know the lawfulness of the Dhamma. Suppose, Lord, a king's frontier fortress was strongly fortified, with strong ramparts and turrets, and it had a single gate, and there was a gatekeeper, intelligent, experienced, and prudent, who would keep out the stranger but allow the friend to enter. As he patrols the path that leads all around the fortress, he does not perceive a hole or fissure in the ramparts even big enough to allow a cat to slip through. So he comes to the conclusion: 'Whatever grosser living things are to enter or leave this city, they will all have to do so just by this gate.' In the same way, Lord, I have come to know the lawfulness of the Dhamma.

"For, Lord, all the Blessed Ones, Arahats, Fully Enlightened Ones of the past had abandoned the five hindrances,[14] the mental defilements that weaken wisdom; had well established their minds in the four foundations of mindfulness;[15] had duly cultivated the seven factors of enlightenment, and were fully enlightened in unsurpassed, supreme Enlightenment.

"And, Lord, all the Blessed Ones, Arahats, Fully Enlightened Ones of the future will abandon the five hindrances, the mental defilements that weaken wisdom; will well establish their minds in the four foundations of mindfulness; will duly cultivate the seven factors of enlightenment, and will be fully enlightened in unsurpassed, supreme Enlightenment.

"And the Blessed One too, Lord, being at present the Arahat, the Fully Enlightened One, has abandoned the five hindrances, the mental defilements that weaken wisdom; has well established his mind in the four foundations of mindfulness; has duly cultivated the seven factors of enlightenment, and is fully enlightened in unsurpassed, supreme Enlightenment."

18. And also in Nālandā, in the mango grove of Pāvārika, the Blessed One often gave counsel to the bhikkhus thus:

"Such and such is virtue; such and such is concentration; and such and such is wisdom. Great becomes the fruit, great is the gain of concentration when it is fully developed by virtuous conduct; great becomes the fruit, great is the gain of wisdom when it is fully developed by concentration; utterly freed from the taints of lust, becoming, and ignorance is the mind that is fully developed in wisdom."

19. When the Blessed One had stayed at Nālandā as long as he pleased, he addressed the Venerable Ānanda thus:

"Come, Ānanda, let us go to Pāṭaligāma."

"So be it, Lord."

And the Blessed One took up his abode at Pāṭaligāma together with a large community of bhikkhus.

20. Then the devotees of Pāṭaligāma came to know: "The Blessed One, they say, has arrived at Pāṭaligāma." And they approached the Blessed One, respectfully greeted him, sat down at one side, and addressed him thus: "May the Blessed One, Lord, kindly visit our council hall." And the Blessed One consented by his silence.

21. Knowing the Blessed One's consent, the devotees of Pāṭaligāma rose from their seats, respectfully saluted him, and keeping their right sides towards him, departed for the council hall. Then they prepared the council hall by covering the floor all over, arranging seats and water, and setting out an oil lamp. Having done this, they returned to the Blessed One, respectfully greeted him, and standing at one side, announced: "Lord, the council hall is ready, with the floor covered all over, seats and water prepared, and an oil

lamp has been set out. Let the Blessed One come, Lord, at his convenience.

22. And the Blessed One got ready, and taking his bowl and robe, went to the council hall together with the company of bhikkhus. After rinsing his feet, the Blessed One entered the council hall and took his seat close to the middle pillar, facing east. The community of bhikkhus, after rinsing their feet, also entered the council hall and took seats near the western wall, facing east, so that the Blessed One was before them. And the devotees of Pāṭaligāma, after rinsing their feet and entering the council hall, sat down near the eastern wall, facing west, so that the Blessed One was in front of them.

The Fruits of an Immoral and a Moral Life

23. Thereupon the Blessed One addressed the devotees of Pāṭaligāma thus: "The immoral man, householders, by falling away from virtue, encounters five perils: great loss of wealth through heedlessness; an evil reputation; a timid and troubled demeanour in every society, be it that of nobles, brahmins, householders, or ascetics; death in bewilderment; and, at the breaking up of the body after death, rebirth in a realm of misery, in an unhappy state, in the nether world, in hell.

24. "Five blessings, householders, accrue to the righteous man through his practice of virtue: great increase of wealth through his diligence; a favourable reputation; a confident deportment, without timidity, in every society, be it that of nobles, brahmins, householders, or ascetics; a serene death; and, at the breaking up of the body after death, rebirth in a happy state, in a heavenly world."

25. And the Blessed One spent much of the night instructing the devotees of Pāṭaligāma in the Dhamma, rousing, edifying, and gladdening them, after which he dismissed them,

saying: "The night is far advanced, householders. You may go at your convenience.

"So be it, Lord." And the devotees of Pāṭaligāma rose from their seats, respectfully saluted the Blessed One, and keeping their right sides towards him, departed. And the Blessed One, soon after their departure, retired into privacy.

26. At that time Sunidha and Vassakāra, the chief ministers of Magadha, were building a fortress at Pāṭaligāma in defence against the Vajjis. And deities in large numbers, counted in thousands, had taken possession of sites at Pāṭaligāma. In the region where deities of great power prevailed, officials of great power were bent on constructing edifices; and where deities of medium power and lesser power prevailed, officials of medium and lesser power were bent on constructing edifices.

27. And the Blessed One saw with the heavenly eye, pure and transcending the faculty of men, the deities, counted in thousands, where they had taken possession of sites in Pāṭaligāma. And rising before the night was spent, towards dawn, the Blessed One addressed the Venerable Ānanda thus: "Who is it, Ānanda, that is erecting a city at Pāṭaligāma?"

"Sunidha and Vassakāra, Lord, the chief ministers of Magadha, are building a fortress at Pāṭaligāma, in defence against the Vajjis."

28. "It is, Ānanda, as if Sunidha and Vassakāra had taken counsel with the gods of the Thirty-three. For I beheld, Ānanda, with the heavenly eye, pure and transcending the faculty of men, a large number of deities, counted in thousands, that have taken possession of sites at Pāṭaligāma. In the region where deities of great power prevail, officials of great power are bent on constructing edifices; and where deities of medium and lesser power prevail, officials of medium and lesser power are bent on constructing edifices.

Truly, Ānanda, as far as the Aryan race extends and trade routes spread, this will be the foremost city Pāṭaliputta, a trade-centre.[16] But Pāṭaliputta, Ānanda, will be assailed by three perils—fire, water, and dissension."

29. Then Sunidha and Vassakāra went to the Blessed One, and after courteous greeting to the Blessed One, and exchanging many pleasant words, they stood at one side and addressed him thus: "May the Venerable Gotama please accept our invitation for tomorrow's meal, together with the community of bhikkhus." And the Blessed One consented by his silence.

30. Knowing the Blessed One's consent, Sunidha and Vassakāra departed for their own abodes, where they had choice food, hard and soft, prepared. And when it was time, they announced to the Blessed One: "It is time, Venerable Gotama; the meal is ready."

Thereupon the Blessed One got ready in the forenoon, and taking bowl and robe, he went together with the community of bhikkhus to the abode of Sunidha and Vassakāra, where he took the seat prepared for him. And Sunidha and Vassakāra themselves attended on the community of bhikkhus headed by the Buddha, and served them with choice food, hard and soft. When the Blessed One had finished his meal and had removed his hand from the bowl, they took low seats and sat down at one side.

31. And the Blessed One thanked them with these stanzas:

"Wherever he may dwell, the prudent man
Ministers to the chaste and virtuous;
And having to these worthy ones made gifts,
He shares his merits with the local devas.

And so revered, they honour him in turn,
Are gracious to him even as a mother
Is towards her own, her only son;
And he who thus enjoys the devas' grace,
And is by them beloved, good fortune sees."

After this, the Blessed One rose from his seat and departed.

Crossing the Ganges

32. Then Sunidha and Vassakāra followed behind the Blessed One, step by step, saying: "Through whichever gate the recluse Gotama will depart today, that we will name the Gotama-gate; and the ford by which he will cross the river Ganges shall be named the Gotama-ford." And so it came to pass, where the gate was concerned.

33. But when the Blessed One came to the river Ganges, it was full to the brim, so that crows could drink from it. And some people went in search of a boat or float, while others tied up a raft, because they desired to get across. But the Blessed One, as quickly as a strong man might stretch out his bent arm or draw in his outstretched arm, vanished from this side of the river Ganges, and came to stand on the yonder side.

34. And the Blessed One saw the people who desired to cross searching for a boat or float, while others were binding rafts. And then the Blessed One, seeing them thus, gave forth the solemn utterance:

"They who have bridged the ocean vast,
Leaving the lowlands far behind,
While others still their frail rafts bind,
Are saved by wisdom unsurpassed."

Part Two
The Journey to Vesālī

The Four Noble Truths

1. Now the Blessed One spoke to the Venerable Ānanda, saying: "Come, Ānanda, let us go to Koṭigāma."

"So be it, Lord." And the Blessed One took up his abode at Koṭigāma together with a large community of bhikkhus.

2. And the Blessed One addressed the bhikkhus, saying: "Bhikkhus, it is through not realizing, through not penetrating the Four Noble Truths that this long course of birth and death has been passed through and undergone by me as well as by you. What are these four? They are the noble truth of suffering; the noble truth of the origin of suffering; the noble truth of the cessation of suffering; and the noble truth of the way to the cessation of suffering. But now, bhikkhus, that these have been realized and penetrated, cut off is the craving for existence, destroyed is that which leads to renewed becoming, and there is no fresh becoming."

3. Thus it was said by the Blessed One. And the Happy One, the Master, further said:

> "Through not seeing the Four Noble Truths,
> Long was the weary path from birth to birth.
> When these are known, removed is rebirth's cause,
> The root of sorrow plucked; then ends rebirth."

4. And also at Koṭigāma the Blessed One often gave counsel to the bhikkhus thus: "Such and such is virtue; such and

such is concentration; and such and such is wisdom. Great becomes the fruit, great is the gain of concentration when it is fully developed by virtuous conduct; great becomes the fruit, great is the gain of wisdom when it is fully developed by concentration; utterly freed from the taints of lust, becoming, and ignorance is the mind that is fully developed in wisdom."

5. When the Blessed One had stayed at Koṭigāma as long as he pleased, he spoke to the Venerable Ānanda, saying: "Come, Ānanda, let us go to Nādikā."

"So be it, Lord." And the Blessed One took up his abode in Nādikā together with a large community of bhikkhus, staying in the Brick House.

The Four Specific Attainments

6. Then the Venerable Ānanda approached the Blessed One and, after greeting him respectfully, sat down at one side. And he said to the Blessed One: "Here in Nādikā, Lord, there have passed away the bhikkhu Sāḷha and the bhikkhunī Nandā. Likewise there have passed away the layman Sudatta and the laywoman Sujātā; likewise the layman Kakudha, Kāliṅga, Nikaṭa, Kaṭissabha, Tuṭṭha, Santuṭṭha, Bhadda, and Subhadda. What is their destiny, Lord? What is their future state?"

7. "The bhikkhu Sāḷha, Ānanda, through the destruction of the taints in this very lifetime has attained to the taint-free deliverance of mind and deliverance through wisdom, having directly known and realized it by himself.[17]

"The bhikkhunī Nandā, Ānanda, through the destruction of the five lower fetters (that bind beings to the world of the senses), has arisen spontaneously (among the Suddhāvāsa deities) and will come to final cessation in that very place, not liable to return from that world.

"The layman Sudatta, Ānanda, through the destruction of the three fetters (self-belief, doubt, and faith in the efficacy of rituals and observances), and the lessening of lust, hatred, and delusion, has become a once-returner and is bound to make an end of suffering after having returned but once more to this world.

"The laywoman Sujātā, Ānanda, through the destruction of the three fetters has become a stream-enterer, and is safe from falling into the states of misery, assured, and bound for Enlightenment.

"The layman Kakudha, Ānanda, through the destruction of the five lower fetters (that bind beings to the world of the senses), has arisen spontaneously (among the Suddhāvāsa deities), and will come to final cessation in that very place, not liable to return from that world.

"So it is with Kāliṅga, Nikaṭa, Kaṭissabha, Tuṭṭha, Santuṭṭha, Bhadda, and Subhadda, and with more than fifty laymen in Nādikā. More than ninety laymen who have passed away in Nādikā, Ānanda, through the destruction of the three fetters, and the lessening of lust, hatred, and delusion, have become once-returners and are bound to make an end of suffering after having returned but once more to this world.

"More than five hundred laymen who have passed away in Nādikā, Ānanda, through the complete destruction of the three fetters have become stream-enterers, and are safe from falling into the states of misery, assured, and bound for Enlightenment.

The Mirror of the Dhamma

8. "But truly, Ānanda, it is nothing strange that human beings should die. But if each time it happens you should come to the Tathāgata and ask about them in this manner,

indeed it would be troublesome to him. Therefore, Ānanda, I will give you the teaching called the Mirror of the Dhamma, possessing which the noble disciple, should he so desire, can declare of himself: 'There is no more rebirth for me in hell, nor as an animal or ghost, nor in any realm of woe. A stream-enterer am I, safe from falling into the states of misery, assured am I and bound for Enlightenment.' "

9. "And what, Ānanda, is that teaching called the Mirror of Dhamma, possessing which the noble disciple may thus declare of himself?

"In this case, Ānanda, the noble disciple possesses unwavering faith in the Buddha thus: 'The Blessed One is an Arahat, the Fully Enlightened One, perfect in knowledge and conduct, the Happy One, the knower of the world, the paramount trainer of beings, the teacher of gods and men, the Enlightened One, the Blessed One.'

"He possesses unwavering faith in the Dhamma thus: 'Well propounded by the Blessed One is the Dhamma, evident, timeless,[18] inviting investigation, leading to emancipation, to be comprehended by the wise, each for himself.'

"He possesses unwavering faith in the Blessed One's Order of Disciples thus: 'Well faring is the Blessed One's Order of Disciples, righteously, wisely, and dutifully: that is to say, the four pairs of men, the eight classes of persons. The Blessed One's Order of Disciples is worthy of honour, of hospitality, of offerings, of veneration—the supreme field for meritorious deeds in the world.'

"And he possesses virtues that are dear to the Noble Ones, complete and perfect, spotless and pure, which are liberating, praised by the wise, uninfluenced (by worldly concerns), and favourable to concentration of mind.

10. "This, Ānanda, is the teaching called the Mirror of the Dhamma, whereby the noble disciple may thus know of him-

self: 'There is no more rebirth for me in hell, nor as an animal or ghost, nor in any realm of woe. A stream-enterer am I, safe from falling into the states of misery, assured am I and bound for Enlightenment.'"

11. And also in Nādikā, in the Brick House, the Blessed One often gave counsel to the bhikkhus thus: "Such and such is virtue; such and such is concentration; and such and such is wisdom. Great becomes the fruit, great is the gain of concentration when it is fully developed by virtuous conduct; great becomes the fruit, great is the gain of wisdom when it is fully developed by concentration; utterly freed from the taints of lust, becoming, and ignorance is the mind that is fully developed in wisdom."

12. When the Blessed One had stayed in Nādikā as long as he pleased, he spoke to the Venerable Ānanda, saying: "Come, Ānanda, let us go to Vesālī."

"So be it, O Lord." And the Blessed One took up his abode in Vesālī together with a large community of bhikkhus, and stayed in Ambapālī's grove.

Mindfulness and Clear Comprehension

13. Then the Blessed One addressed the bhikkhus, saying: "Mindful should you dwell, bhikkhus, clearly comprehending; thus I exhort you.

14. "And how, bhikkhus, is a bhikkhu mindful? When he dwells contemplating the body in the body, earnestly, clearly comprehending, and mindfully, after having overcome desire and sorrow in regard to the world; and when he dwells contemplating feelings in feelings, the mind in the mind, and mental objects in mental objects, earnestly, clearly comprehending, and mindfully, after having overcome desire and sorrow in regard to the world, then is he said to be mindful.

15. "And how, bhikkhus, does a bhikkhu have clear comprehension? When he remains fully aware of his coming and going, his looking forward and his looking away, his bending and stretching, his wearing of his robe and carrying of his bowl, his eating and drinking, masticating and savouring, his defecating and urinating, his walking, standing, sitting, lying down, going to sleep or keeping awake, his speaking or being silent, then is he said to have clear comprehension.

"Mindful should you dwell, bhikkhus, clearly comprehending; thus I exhort you."

Ambapālī and the Licchavis

16. Then Ambapālī the courtesan came to know: "The Blessed One, they say, has arrived at Vesālī and is now staying in my Mango Grove." And she ordered a large number of magnificient carriages to be made ready, mounted one of them herself, and accompanied by the rest, drove out from Vesālī towards her park. She went by carriage as far as the carriage could go, then alighted; and approaching the Blessed One on foot, she respectfully greeted him and sat down at one side. And the Blessed One instructed Ambapālī the courtesan in the Dhamma and roused, edified, and gladdened her.

17. Thereafter Ambapālī the courtesan spoke to the Blessed One, saying: "May the Blessed One, O Lord, please accept my invitation for tomorrow's meal, together with the community of bhikkhus." And by his silence the Blessed One consented.

Sure, then, of the Blessed One's consent, Ambapālī the courtesan rose from her seat, respectfully saluted him, and keeping her right side towards him, took her departure.

18. Then the Licchavis of Vesālī came to know: "The Blessed One, they say, has arrived at Vesālī and is now staying in Ambapālī's grove." And they ordered a large number of magnificient carriages to be made ready, each mounted one, and accompanied by the rest, drove out from Vesālī. Now, of these Licchavis, some were in blue, with clothing and ornaments all of blue, while others were in yellow, red, and white.

19. And it so happened that Ambapālī the courtesan drove up against the young Licchavis, axle by axle, wheel by wheel, and yoke by yoke. Thereupon the Licchavis exclaimed: "Why do you drive up against us in this fashion, Ambapālī?"

"Thus it is, indeed, my princes, and not otherwise! For the Blessed One is invited by me for tomorrow's meal, together with the community of bhikkhus!"

"Give up the meal, Ambapālī, for a hundred thousand!"

But she replied: "Even if you were to give me Vesālī, sirs, together with its tributary lands, I would not give up a meal of such importance."

Then the Licchavis snapped their fingers in annoyance: "See, friends! We are defeated by this mango lass! We are utterly outdone by this mango lass!" But they continued on their way to Ambapālī's grove.

20. And the Blessed One beheld the Licchavis from afar, as they drove up. Then he spoke to the bhikkhus, saying: "Those of you, bhikkhus, who have not yet seen the Thirty-three gods, may behold the assembly of the Licchavis, and may gaze on them, for they are comparable to the assembly of the Thirty-three gods."

21. Then the Licchavis drove their carriages as far as the carriages could go, then alighted; and approaching the Blessed One on foot, they respectfully greeted him and sat down at one side. The Blessed One instructed the Licchavis in the Dhamma, and roused, edified, and gladdened them.

22. Thereafter the Licchavis spoke to the Blessed One, saying: "May the Blessed One, O Lord, please accept our invitation for tomorrow's meal, together with the community of bhikkhus."

"The invitation for tomorrow's meal, Licchavis, has been accepted by me from Ambapālī the courtesan."

Then the Licchavis snapped their fingers in annoyance: "See, friends! We are defeated by this mango lass! We are utterly outdone by this mango lass!" And then the Licchavis, approving of the Blessed One's words and delighted with them, rose from their seats, respectfully saluted him, and keeping their right sides towards him, took their departure.

23. Then, after the night had passed, Ambapālī the courtesan had choice food, hard and soft, prepared in her park, and announced it to the Blessed One: "It is time, O Lord; the meal is ready." Thereupon the Blessed One got ready in the forenoon, and taking bowl and robe, he went together with the community of bhikkhus to Ambapālī's dwelling, and there he took the seat prepared for him. And Ambapālī herself attended on the community of bhikkhus headed by the Buddha, and served them with choice food, hard and soft.

24. And when the Blessed One had finished his meal and had removed his hand from his bowl, Ambapālī the courtesan took a low seat, and placing herself at one side, spoke to the Blessed One, saying: "This park, O Lord, I offer to the community of bhikkhus headed by the Buddha." And the Blessed One accepted the park. He then instructed Ambapālī in the Dhamma, and having roused, edified, and gladdened her, he rose from his seat and departed.

25. And also at Vesālī, in Ambapālī's grove, the Blessed One often gave counsel to the bhikkhus thus: "Such and such is virtue; such and such is concentration; and such and such

is wisdom. Great becomes the fruit, great is the gain of concentration when it is fully developed by virtuous conduct; great becomes the fruit, great is the gain of wisdom when it is fully developed by concentration; utterly freed from the taints of lust, becoming, and ignorance is the mind that is fully developed in wisdom."

26. When the Blessed One had stayed in Ambapālī's grove as long as he pleased, he spoke to the Venerable Ānanda, saying: "Come, Ānanda, let us go to the village of Beluva."

"So be it, Lord." And the Blessed One took up his abode in the village of Beluva together with a large community of bhikkhus.

The Blessed One's Deadly Sickness

27. At that time the Blessed One spoke to the bhikkhus, saying: "Go now, bhikkhus, and seek shelter anywhere in the neighbourhood of Vesālī where you are welcome, among acquaintances and friends, and there spend the rainy season. As for me, I shall spend the rainy season in this very place, in the village of Beluva."

"So be it, O Lord," the bhikkhus said.

28. But when the Blessed One had entered upon the rainy season, there arose in him a severe illness, and sharp and deadly pains came upon him. And the Blessed One endured them mindfully, clearly comprehending and unperturbed.

29. Then it occurred to the Blessed One: "It would not be fitting if I came to my final passing away without addressing those who attended on me, without taking leave of the community of bhikkhus. Then let me suppress this illness by strength of will, resolve to maintain the life process, and live on."

30. And the Blessed One suppressed the illness by strength

of will, resolved to maintain the life process, and lived on. So it came about that the Blessed One's illness was allayed.

31. And the Blessed One recovered from that illness; and soon after his recovery he came out from his dwelling place and sat down in the shade of the building, on a seat prepared for him. Then the Venerable Ānanda approached the Blessed One, respectfully greeted him, and sitting down at one side, he spoke to the Blessed One, saying: "Fortunate it is for me, O Lord, to see the Blessed One at ease again! Fortunate it is for me, O Lord, to see the Blessed One recovered! For truly, Lord, when I saw the Blessed One's sickness it was as though my own body became weak as a creeper, every thing around became dim to me, and my senses failed me. Yet, Lord, I still had some little comfort in the thought that the Blessed One would not come to his final passing away until he had given some last instructions respecting the community of bhikkhus."

32. Thus spoke the Venerable Ānanda, but the Blessed One answered him, saying: "What more does the community of bhikkhus expect from me, Ānanda? I have set forth the Dhamma without making any distinction of esoteric and exoteric doctrine; there is nothing, Ānanda, with regard to the teachings that the Tathāgata holds to the last with the closed fist of a teacher who keeps some things back. Whosoever may think that it is he who should lead the community of bhikkhus, or that the community depends upon him, it is such a one that would have to give last instructions respecting them. But, Ānanda, the Tathāgata has no such idea as that it is he who should lead the community of bhikkhus, or that the community depends upon him. So what instructions should he have to give respecting the community of bhikkhus?

"Now I am frail, Ānanda, old, aged, far gone in years. This is my eightieth year, and my life is spent. Even as an old cart, Ānanda, is held together with much difficulty, so the body of the Tathāgata is kept going only with supports. It is, Ānanda, only when the Tathāgata, disregarding external objects, with the cessation of certain feelings, attains to and abides in the signless concentration of mind,[19] that his body is more comfortable.

33. "Therefore, Ānanda, be islands unto yourselves, refuges unto yourselves, seeking no external refuge; with the Dhamma as your island, the Dhamma as your refuge, seeking no other refuge.

"And how, Ānanda, is a bhikkhu an island unto himself, a refuge unto himself, seeking no external refuge; with the Dhamma as his island, the Dhamma as his refuge, seeking no other refuge?

34. "When he dwells contemplating the body in the body, earnestly, clearly comprehending, and mindfully, after having overcome desire and sorrow in regard to the world; when he dwells contemplating feelings in feelings, the mind in the mind, and mental objects in mental objects, earnestly, clearly comprehending, and mindfully, after having overcome desire and sorrow in regard to the world, then, truly, he is an island unto himself, a refuge unto himself, seeking no external refuge; having the Dhamma as his island, the Dhamma as his refuge, seeking no other refuge.

35. "Those bhikkhus of mine, Ānanda, who now or after I am gone, abide as an island unto themselves, as a refuge unto themselves, seeking no other refuge; having the Dhamma as their island and refuge, seeking no other refuge: it is they who will become the highest,[20] if they have the desire to learn."

Part Three
Relinquishing the Will to Live

The Blessed One's Prompting

1. Then the Blessed One, getting ready in the forenoon, took bowl and robe and went into Vesālī for alms. After the alms round and meal, on his return, he spoke to the Venerable Ānanda, saying: "Take up a mat, Ānanda, and let us spend the day at the Cāpāla shrine."

"So be it, Lord." And the Venerable Ānanda took up a mat and followed behind the Blessed One, step by step.

2. And the Blessed One went to the Cāpāla shrine and sat down on the seat prepared for him. And when the Venerable Ānanda had seated himself at one side after he had respectfully saluted the Blessed One, the Lord said to him: "Pleasant, Ānanda, is Vesālī; pleasant are the shrines of Udena, Gotamaka, Sattambaka, Bahuputta, Sarandada, and Cāpāla."

3. And the Blessed One said: "Whosoever, Ānanda, has developed, practised, employed, strengthened, maintained, scrutinized, and brought to perfection the four constituents of psychic power could, if he so desired, remain throughout a world-period or until the end of it.[21] The Tathāgata, Ānanda, has done so. Therefore the Tathāgata could, if he so desired, remain throughout a world-period or until the end of it."

4. But the Venerable Ānanda was unable to grasp the plain suggestion, the significant prompting, given by the Blessed One. As though his mind was influenced by Māra,[22] he did

not beseech the Blessed One: "May the Blessed One remain, O Lord! May the Happy One remain, O Lord, throughout the world-period, for the welfare and happiness of the multitude, out of compassion for the world, for the benefit, well being, and happiness of gods and men!"

5. And when for a second and a third time the Blessed One repeated his words, the Venerable Ānanda remained silent.

6. Then the Blessed One said to the Venerable Ānanda: "Go now, Ānanda, and do as seems fit to you."

"Even so, O Lord." And the Venerable Ānanda, rising from his seat, respectfully saluted the Blessed One, and keeping his right side towards him, took his seat under a tree some distance away.

Māra's Appeal

7. And when the Venerable Ānanda had gone away, Māra, the Evil One, approached the Blessed One. And standing at one side he spoke to the Blessed One, saying: "Now, O Lord, let the Blessed One come to his final passing away; let the Happy One utterly pass away! The time has come for the Parinibbāna of the Lord.

"For the Blessed One, O Lord, spoke these words to me: 'I shall not come to my final passing away, Evil One, until my bhikkhus and bhikkhunis, laymen and laywomen, have come to be true disciples—wise, well disciplined, apt and learned, preservers of the Dhamma, living according to the Dhamma, abiding by the appropriate conduct, and having learned the Master's word, are able to expound it, preach it, proclaim it, establish it, reveal it, explain it in detail, and make it clear; until, when adverse opinions arise, they shall be able to refute them thoroughly and well, and to preach this convincing and liberating Dhamma.'[23]

8. "And now, O Lord, bhikkhus and bhikkhunīs, laymen and laywomen, have become the Blessed One's disciples in just this way. So, O Lord, let the Blessed One come to his final passing away! The time has come for the Parinibbāna of the Lord.

"For the Blessed One, O Lord, spoke these words to me: 'I shall not come to my final passing away, Evil One, until this holy life taught by me has become successful, prosperous, far-renowned, popular, and widespread, until it is well proclaimed among gods and men.' And this too has come to pass in just this way. So, O Lord, let the Blessed One come to his final passing away, let the Happy One utterly pass away! The time has come for the Parinibbāna of the Lord."

The Blessed One Relinquishes His Will to Live

9. When this was said, the Blessed One spoke to Māra, the Evil One, saying: "Do not trouble yourself, Evil One. Before long the Parinibbāna of the Tathāgata will come about. Three months hence the Tathāgata will utterly pass away."

10. And at the Cāpāla shrine the Blessed One thus mindfully and clearly comprehending renounced his will to live on. And upon the Lord's renouncing his will to live on, there came a tremendous earthquake, dreadful and astonishing, and thunder rolled across the heavens. And the Blessed One beheld it with understanding, and made this solemn utterance:

> "What causes life, unbounded or confined[24]—
> His process of becoming[25]—this the Sage
> Renounces. With inward calm and joy he breaks,
> As though a coat of mail, his own life's cause."[26]

11. Then it came to the mind of the Venerable Ānanda: "Marvellous it is indeed, and most wonderful! The earth

shakes mightily, tremendously! Dreadful and astonishing it is, how the thunders roll across the heavens! What could be the reason, what the cause, that so mighty an earthquake should arise?"

Eight Causes of Earthquakes

12. And the Venerable Ānanda approached the Blessed One, and respectfully greeting him, sat down at one side. Then he spoke to the Blessed One, saying: "Marvellous it is indeed, and most wonderful! The earth shakes mightily, tremendously! Dreadful and astonishing it is how the thunders roll across the heavens! What could be the reason, what the cause, that so mighty an earthquake should arise?"

13. Then the Blessed One said: "There are eight reasons, Ānanda, eight causes for a mighty earthquake to arise. What are those eight?

14. "This great earth, Ānanda, is established upon liquid, the liquid upon the atmosphere, and the atmosphere upon space. And when, Ānanda, mighty atmospheric disturbances take place, the liquid is agitated. And with the agitation of the liquid, tremors of the earth arise. This is the first reason, the first cause for the arising of mighty earthquakes.

15. "Again, Ānanda, when an ascetic or holy man of great power, one who has gained mastery of his mind, or a deity who is mighty and potent, develops intense concentration on the delimited aspect of the earth element, and to a boundless degree on the liquid element, he, too, causes the earth to tremble, quiver, and shake. This is the second reason, the second cause for the arising of mighty earthquakes.

16–21. "Again, Ānanda, when the Bodhisatta departs from the Tusita realm and descends into his mother's womb, mindfully and clearly comprehending; and when the Bodhisatta comes out from his mother's womb, mindfully and clearly comprehending; and when the Tathāgata becomes fully enlightened in unsurpased, supreme Enlightenment; when the Tathāgata sets rolling the excellent Wheel of the Dhamma; when the Tathāgata renounces his will to live on; and when the Tathāgata comes to pass away into the state of Nibbāna in which no element of clinging remains—then, too, Ānanda, this great earth trembles, quivers, and shakes.

"These, Ānanda, are the eight reasons, the eight causes for a great earthquake to arise.[27]

Eight Assemblies

22. "Now there are eight kinds of assemblies, Ānanda, that is to say, assemblies of nobles, brahmins, householders, ascetics, of the Four Great Kings, of the Thirty-three gods, of Māras, and of Brahmās.

23. "And I recall, Ānanda, how I have attended each of these eight kinds of assemblies, amounting to hundreds.[28] And before seating myself and starting the conversation or the discussion, I made my appearance resemble theirs, my voice resemble theirs. And so I taught them the Dhamma, and roused, edified, and gladdened them. Yet while I was speaking to them thus, they did not know me, and they would enquire of one another, asking: 'Who is he that speaks to us? Is it a man or a god?'

"Then having taught them the Dhamma, and roused, edified, and gladdened them, I would straightaway vanish. And when I had vanished, too, they did not know me, and they would enquire of one another, asking: 'Who is he that has vanished? Is it a man or a god?'

"And such, Ānanda, are the eight kinds of assemblies.

Eight Fields of Mastery

24. "Now there are eight fields of mastery,[29] Ānanda. What are those eight?

25. "When one, perceiving forms subjectively,[30] sees small forms, beautiful or ugly, external to himself,[31] and mastering them, is aware that he perceives and knows them as they are—this is the first field of mastery.

26. "When one, perceiving forms subjectively, sees large forms, beautiful or ugly, external to himself, and mastering them, is aware that he perceives and knows them as they are—this is the second field of mastery.

27. "When one, not perceiving forms subjectively,[32] sees small forms, beautiful or ugly, external to himself, and mastering them, is aware that he perceives and knows them as they are—this is the third field of mastery.

28. "When one, not perceiving forms subjectively, sees large forms, beautiful or ugly, external to himself, and mastering them, is aware that he perceives and knows them as they are—this is the fourth field of mastery.

29. "When one, not perceiving forms subjectively, sees forms external to himself that are blue, blue in colour, of a blue lustre like the blossoms of flax, or like fine Benares muslin which, burnished on both sides, is blue, blue in colour, of a blue lustre—when such a one sees forms external to himself that are blue, and mastering them, is aware that he perceives and knows them as they are—this is the fifth field of mastery.

30. "When one, not perceiving forms subjectively, sees forms external to himself that are yellow, yellow in colour, of a yellow lustre like the Kanikāra blossom, or like fine Benares muslin which, burnished on both sides, is yellow, yellow in colour, of a yellow lustre—when such a one sees

forms external to himself that are yellow, and mastering them, is aware that he perceives and knows them as they are—this is the sixth field of mastery.

31. "When one, not perceiving forms subjectively, sees forms external to himself that are red, red in colour, of a red lustre like the Bandhujīvaka blossom, or like fine Benares muslin which, burnished on both sides, is red, red in colour, of a red lustre—when such a one sees forms external to himself that are red, and mastering them, is aware that he perceives and knows them as they are—this is the seventh field of mastery.

32. "When one, not perceiving forms subjectively, sees forms external to himself that are white, white in colour, of a white lustre like the morning star, or like fine Benares muslin which, burnished on both sides, is white, white in colour, of a white lustre—when such a one sees forms external to himself that are white, and mastering them, is aware that he perceives and knows them as they are—this is the eighth field of mastery.

"These, Ānanda, are the eight fields of mastery.

Eight Liberations

33. "Now there are eight liberations, Ānanda. What are those eight?[33]

34. "Oneself having form,[34] one perceives forms; this is the first liberation.

35. "Being unaware of one's own form, one perceives forms external to oneself; this is the second liberation.

36. "Experiencing loveliness, one is intent upon it;[35] this is the third liberation.

37. "By utterly transcending the perceptions of matter, by the disappearance of the perceptions of sense-reaction, and

by giving no attention to diversity-perceptions, one becomes aware of, attains to, and abides in the sphere of infinite space; this is the fourth liberation.

38. "By utterly transcending the sphere of infinite space, one becomes aware of, attains to, and abides in the sphere of infinite consciousness; this is the fifth liberation.

39. "By utterly transcending the sphere of infinite consciousness, one becomes aware of, attains to, and abides in the sphere of nothingness; this is the sixth liberation.

40. "By utterly transcending the sphere of nothingness, one attains to and abides in the sphere of neither-perception-nor-non-perception; this is the seventh liberation.

41. "By utterly transcending the sphere of neither-perception-nor-non-perception, one attains to and abides in the cessation of perception and sensation; this is the eighth liberation.

"These, Ānanda, are the eight liberations.

Māra's Former Temptation

42. "There was a time, Ānanda, when I dwelt at Uruvelā, on the bank of the Nerañjarā River, at the foot of the goatherds' banyan-tree, soon after my supreme Enlightenment. And Māra, the Evil One, approached me, saying: 'Now, O Lord, let the Blessed One come to his final passing away! Let the Happy One utterly pass away! The time has come for the Parinibbāna of the Lord.'

43. "Then, Ānanda, I answered Māra, the Evil One, saying: 'I shall not come to my final passing away, Evil One, until my bhikkhus and bhikkhunīs, laymen and laywomen, have come to be true disciples—wise, well disciplined, apt and learned, preservers of the Dhamma, living according to the Dhamma, abiding by appropriate conduct and, having

learned the Master's word, are able to expound it, preach it, proclaim it, establish it, reveal it, explain it in detail, and make it clear; until, when adverse opinions arise, they shall be able to refute them thoroughly and well, and to preach this convincing and liberating Dhamma.

44. 'I shall not come to my final passing away, Evil One, until this holy life taught by me has become successful, prosperous, far-renowned, popular, and widespread, until it is well proclaimed among gods and men.'

45. "And again today, Ānanda, at the Cāpāla shrine, Māra, the Evil One, approached me, saying: 'Now, O Lord, bhikkhus and bhikkhunīs, laymen and laywomen, have come to be true disciples of the Blessed One—wise, well disciplined, apt and learned, preservers of the Dhamma, living according to the Dhamma, abiding in the appropriate conduct, and having learned the Master's word, are able to expound it, preach it, proclaim it, establish it, reveal it, explain it in detail, and make it clear; and when adverse opinions arise, they are now able to refute them thoroughly and well, and to preach this convincing and liberating Dhamma.

'And now, O Lord, this holy life taught by the Blessed One has become successful, prosperous, far-renowned, popular and widespread, and it is well proclaimed among gods and men. Therefore, O Lord, let the Blessed One come to his final passing away! Let the Happy One utterly pass away! The time has come for the Parinibbāna of the Lord.'

46. "And then, Ānanda, I answered Māra, the Evil One, saying: 'Do not trouble yourself, Evil One. Before long the Parinibbāna of the Tathāgata will come about. Three months hence the Tathāgata will utterly pass away.'

47. "And in this way, Ānanda, today at the Cāpāla shrine the Tathāgata has renounced his will to live on."

Ānanda's Appeal

48. At these words the Venerable Ānanda spoke to the Blessed One, saying: "May the Blessed One remain, O Lord! May the Happy One remain, O Lord, throughout the world-period, for the welfare and happiness of the multitude, out of compassion for the world, for the benefit, well being, and happiness of gods and men!"

49. And the Blessed One answered, saying: "Enough, Ānanda. Do not entreat the Tathāgata, for the time is past, Ānanda, for such an entreaty."

50–51. But for a second and a third time, the Venerable Ānanda said to the Blessed One: "May the Blessed One remain, O Lord! May the Happy One remain, O Lord, throughout the world-period, for the welfare and happiness of the multitude, out of compassion for the world, for the benefit, well being, and happiness of gods and men!"

52. Then the Blessed One said: "Do you have faith, Ānanda, in the Enlightenment of the Tathāgata?" And the Venerable Ānanda replied: "Yes, O Lord, I do."

"Then how, Ānanda, can you persist against the Tathāgata even up to the third time?"

53. Then the Venerable Ānanda said: "This, O Lord, I have heard and learned from the Blessed One himself when the Blessed One said to me: 'Whosoever, Ānanda, has developed, practised, employed, strengthened, maintained, scrutinized, and brought to perfection the four constituents of psychic power could, if he so desired, remain throughout a world-period or until the end of it. The Tathāgata, Ānanda, has done so. Therefore the Tathāgata could, if he so desired, remain throughout a world-period or until the end of it.' "

54. "And did you believe it, Ānanda?"

"Yes, O Lord, I did."

"Then, Ānanda, the fault is yours. Herein have you failed, inasmuch as you were unable to grasp the plain suggestion, the significant prompting given by the Tathāgata, and you did not then entreat the Tathāgata to remain. For if you had done so, Ānanda, twice the Tathāgata might have declined, but the third time he would have consented. Therefore, Ānanda, the fault is yours; herein have you failed.

55. "At Rājagaha, Ānanda, when dwelling at Vultures' Peak, I spoke to you, saying: 'Pleasant, Ānanda, is Rājagaha; pleasant is Vultures' Peak. Whosoever, Ānanda, has developed ... Therefore the Tathāgata could, if he so desired, remain throughout a world-period or until the end of it.'

56. "So also at the Banyan Grove, at Robbers' Cliff, at the Sattapaṇṇi Cave on the Vebhāra Mountain, at the Black Rock of Isigili, at the Serpents' Pool in the Cool Forest, at the Tapoda Grove, at the Bamboo Grove in the Squirrels' Feeding-ground, at Jīvaka's Mango Grove, and at Small Nook in the Deer Park I spoke to you in the same words, saying: 'Pleasant, Ānanda, is Rājagaha, pleasant are these places. Whosoever, Ānanda, has developed ... Therefore the Tathāgata could, if he so desired, remain throughout a world-period or until the end of it.'

"But you, Ānanda, were unable to grasp the plain suggestion, the significant prompting given you by the Tathāgata, and you did not entreat the Tathāgata to remain. For if you had done so, Ānanda, twice the Tathāgata might have declined, but the third time he would have consented. Therefore, Ānanda, the fault is yours; herein you have failed.

57. "So also at Vesāli, Ānanda, at different times the Tathāgata has spoken to you, saying: 'Pleasant, Ānanda, is Vesāli; pleasant are the shrines of Udena, Gotamaka, Sattambaka, Bahuputta, Sarandada, and Cāpāla. Whosoever, Ānanda, has developed ... Therefore the Tathāgata could, if

he so desired, remain throughout a world-period or until the end of it.'

"But you, Ānanda, were unable to grasp the plain suggestion, the significant prompting, given you by the Tathāgata, and you did not entreat the Tathāgata to remain. For if you had done so, Ānanda, twice the Tathāgata might have declined, but the third time he would have consented. Therefore, Ānanda, the fault is yours; herein you have failed.

58. "Yet, Ānanda, have I not taught from the very beginning that with all that is dear and beloved there must be change, separation, and severance? Of that which is born, come into being, is compounded and subject to decay, how can one say: 'May it not come to dissolution!' There can be no such state of things. And of that, Ānanda, which the Tathāgata has finished with, that which he has relinquished, given up, abandoned, and rejected—his will to live on—the Tathāgata's word has been spoken once for all: 'Before long the Parinibbāna of the Tathāgata will come about. Three months hence the Tathāgata will utterly pass away.' And that the Tathāgata should withdraw his words for the sake of living on—this is an impossibility.

The Last Admonition

59. "So, then, Ānanda, let us go to the hall of the Gabled House, in the Great Forest." And the Venerable Ānanda replied: "So be it, Lord."

60. Then the Blessed One, with the Venerable Ānanda, went to the hall of the Gabled House, in the Great Forest. And there he spoke to the Venerable Ānanda, saying: "Go now, Ānanda, and assemble in the hall of audience all the bhikkhus who dwell in the neighbourhood of Vesālī."

"So be it, Lord." And the Venerable Ānanda gathered all

the bhikkhus who dwelt in the neighbourhood of Vesālī, and assembled them in the hall of audience. And then, respectfully saluting the Blessed One, and standing at one side, he said: "The community of bhikkhus is assembled, Lord. Now let the Blessed One do as he wishes."

61. Thereupon the Blessed One entered the hall of audience, and taking the seat prepared for him, he exhorted the bhikkhus, saying: "Now, O bhikkhus, I say to you that these teachings of which I have direct knowledge and which I have made known to you—these you should thoroughly learn, cultivate, develop, and frequently practise, that the life of purity may be established and may long endure, for the welfare and happiness of the multitude, out of compassion for the world, for the benefit, well being, and happiness of gods and men.

62. "And what, bhikkhus, are these teachings? They are the four foundations of mindfulness, the four right efforts, the four constituents of psychic power, the five faculties, the five powers, the seven factors of enlightenment, and the Noble Eightfold Path. These, bhikkhus, are the teachings of which I have direct knowledge, which I have made known to you, and which you should thoroughly learn, cultivate, develop, and frequently practise, that the life of purity may be established and may long endure, for the welfare and happiness of the multitude, out of compassion for the world, for the benefit, well being, and happiness of gods and men."

63. Then the Blessed One said to the bhikkhus: "So, bhikkhus, I exhort you: All compounded things are subject to vanish. Strive with earnestness. The time of the Tathāgata's Parinibbāna is near. Three months hence the Tathāgata will utterly pass away."

64. And having spoken these words, the Happy One, the Master, spoke again, saying:

"My years are now full ripe, the life span left is short.
Departing, I go hence from you, relying on myself
alone.
Be earnest, then, O bhikkhus, be mindful and of
virtue pure!
With firm resolve, guard your own mind!
Whoso untiringly pursues the Dhamma and the
Discipline
Shall go beyond the round of births and make an end
of suffering."

PART FOUR
The Last Meal

The Elephant's Look

1. Then the Blessed One, getting ready in the forenoon, took bowl and robe and went into Vesālī for alms. After the alms round and meal, on his return, he looked upon Vesālī with the elephant's look,[36] and said to the Venerable Ānanda: "This, Ānanda, is the last time that the Tathāgata will look upon Vesālī. Come, Ānanda, let us go to Bhandagāma."

"So be it, O Lord." And the Blessed One took up his abode at Bhandagāma together with a large community of bhikkhus.

2. And the Blessed One addressed the bhikkhus, saying: "Bhikkhus, it is through not realizing, through not penetrating four principles that this long course of birth and death has been passed through and undergone by me as well as by you. What are those four? They are: noble virtue, noble concentration, noble wisdom, and noble emancipation. But now, bhikkhus, that these have been realized and penetrated, cut off is the craving for existence, destroyed is that which leads to renewed becoming, and there is no fresh becoming."

3. And having spoken these words, the Happy One, the Master, spoke again, saying:

> "Virtue, concentration, wisdom, and emancipation
> unsurpassed—
> These are the principles realized by Gotama the
> renowned;

And, knowing them, he, the Buddha, to his monks
has taught the Dhamma.
He, the destroyer of suffering, the Master, the Seer, is
at peace."

4. And also at Bhandagāma the Blessed One often gave counsel to the bhikkhus thus: "Such and such is virtue; such and such is concentration; and such and such is wisdom. Great becomes the fruit, great is the gain of concentration when it is fully developed by virtuous conduct; great becomes the fruit, great is the gain of wisdom when it is fully developed by concentration; utterly freed from the taints of lust, becoming, and ignorance is the mind that is fully developed in wisdom."

5. When the Blessed One had stayed at Bhandagāma as long as he pleased, he spoke to the Venerable Ānanda: "Come, Ānanda, let us go to Hatthigāma."

"So be it, Lord." And the Blessed One took up his abode at Hatthigāma together with a large community of bhikkhus.

And when the Blessed One had stayed at Hatthigāma as long as he pleased, he took up his abode at Ambagāma, then at Jambugāma. And at each of these places the Blessed One often gave counsel to the bhikkhus thus: "Such and such is virtue; such and such is concentration; and such and such is wisdom. Great becomes the fruit, great is the gain of concentration when it is fully developed by virtuous conduct; great becomes the fruit, great is the gain of wisdom when it is fully developed by concentration; utterly freed from the taints of lust, becoming, and ignorance is the mind that is fully developed in wisdom."

6. And when the Blessed One had stayed at Jambugāma as long as he pleased, he spoke to the Venerable Ānanda: "Come, Ānanda, let us go to Bhoganagara."

"So be it, Lord." And the Blessed One took up his abode

at Bhoganagara together with a large community of bhikkhus, and stayed in the Ānanda shrine.

The Four Great References

7. And there the Blessed One addressed the bhikkhus, saying: "Now, bhikkhus, I shall make known to you the four great references.[37] Listen and pay heed to my words." And those bhikkhus answered, saying:

"So be it, Lord."

8–11. Then the Blessed One said: "In this fashion, bhikkhus, a bhikkhu might speak: 'Face to face with the Blessed One, brethren, I have heard and learned thus: This is the Dhamma and the Discipline, the Master's Dispensation'; or: 'In an abode of such and such a name lives a community with elders and a chief. Face to face with that community, I have heard and learned thus: This is the Dhamma and the Discipline, the Master's Dispensation'; or: 'In an abode of such and such a name live several bhikkhus who are elders, who are learned, who have accomplished their course, who are preservers of the Dhamma, the Discipline, and the Summaries. Face to face with those elders, I have heard and learned thus: This is the Dhamma and the Discipline, the Master's Dispensation'; or: 'In an abode of such and such a name lives a single bhikkhu who is an elder, who is learned, who has accomplished his course, who is a preserver of the Dhamma, the Discipline, and the Summaries. Face to face with that elder, I have heard and learned thus: This is the Dhamma and the Discipline, the Master's Dispensation.'

"In such a case, bhikkhus, the declaration of such a bhikkhu is neither to be received with approval nor with scorn. Without approval and without scorn, but carefully studying the sentences word by word, one should trace them in the Discourses and verify them by the Discipline. If they are neither traceable in the Discourses nor verifiable by the Discipline, one must conclude thus: 'Certainly, this is not the Blessed One's utterance; this has been misunderstood by that bhikkhu—or by that community, or by those elders, or by that elder.' In that way, bhikkhus, you should reject it. But if the sentences concerned are traceable in the Discourses and verifiable by the Discipline, then one must conclude thus: 'Certainly, this is the Blessed One's utterance; this has been well understood by that bhikkhu—or by that community, or by those elders, or by that elder.' And in that way, bhikkhus, you may accept it on the first, second, third, or fourth reference. These, bhikkhus, are the four great references for you to preserve."

12. And also at Bhoganagara, at the Ānanda shrine, the Blessed One often gave counsel to the bhikkhus thus: "Such and such is virtue; such and such is concentration; and such and such is wisdom. Great becomes the fruit, great is the gain of concentration when it is fully developed by virtuous conduct; great becomes the fruit, great is the gain of wisdom when it is fully developed by concentration; utterly freed from the taints of lust, becoming, and ignorance is the mind that is fully developed in wisdom."

13. When the Blessed One had stayed at Bhoganagara as long as he pleased, he spoke to the Venerable Ānanda, saying: "Come, Ānanda, let us go to Pāvā."

"So be it, Lord." And the Blessed One took up his abode at Pāvā together with a great community of bhikkhus, and stayed in the Mango Grove of Cunda, who was by family a metalworker.

The Buddha's Last Meal

14. And Cunda the metalworker came to know: "The Blessed One, they say, has arrived at Pāvā, and is staying in my Mango Grove." And he went to the Blessed One, and having respectfully greeted him, sat down at one side. And the Blessed One instructed Cunda the metalworker in the Dhamma, and roused, edified, and gladdened him.

15. Then Cunda spoke to the Blessed One, saying: "May the Blessed One, O Lord, please accept my invitation for tomorrow's meal, together with the community of bhikkhus." And by his silence the Blessed One consented.

16. Sure, then, of the Blessed One's consent, Cunda the metalworker rose from his seat, respectfully saluted the Blessed One, and keeping his right side towards him, took his departure.

17. And Cunda the metalworker, after the night had passed, had choice food, hard and soft, prepared in his abode, together with a quantity of *sūkara-maddava*,[38] and announced it to the Blessed One, saying: "It is time, O Lord, the meal is ready."

18. Thereupon the Blessed One, in the forenoon, having got ready, took bowl and robe and went with the community of bhikkhus to the house of Cunda, and there sat down on the seat prepared for him. And he spoke to Cunda, saying: "With the *sūkara-maddava* you have prepared, Cunda, you may serve me; with the other food, hard and soft, you may serve the community of bhikkhus."

"So be it, Lord." And with the *sūkara-maddava* prepared by him, he served the Blessed One; and with the other food, hard and soft, he served the community of bhikkhus.

19. Thereafter the Blessed One spoke to Cunda, saying: "Whatever, Cunda, is left over of the *sūkara-maddava*, bury

that in a pit. For I do not see in all this world, with its gods, Māras, and Brahmās, among the host of ascetics and brahmins, gods and men, anyone who could eat it and entirely digest it except the Tathāgata alone."

And Cunda the metalworker answered the Blessed One saying: "So be it, O Lord." And what remained over of the *sūkara-maddava* he buried in a pit.

20. Then he returned to the Blessed One, respectfully greeted him, and sat down at one side. And the Blessed One instructed Cunda the metalworker in the Dhamma, and roused, edified, and gladdened him. After this he rose from his seat and departed.

21. And soon after the Blessed One had eaten the meal provided by Cunda the metalworker, a dire sickness fell upon him, even dysentery, and he suffered sharp and deadly pains. But the Blessed One endured them mindfully, clearly comprehending and unperturbed.

22. Then the Blessed One spoke to the Venerable Ānanda, saying: "Come, Ānanda, let us go to Kusinārā." And the Venerable Ānanda answered: "So be it, Lord."

23. When he had eaten Cunda's food, I heard,
With fortitude the deadly pains he bore.
From the *sūkara-maddava* a sore
And dreadful sickness came upon the Lord.
But nature's pangs he endured. "Come, let us go
To Kusinārā," was his dauntless word.[39]

The Clearing of the Waters

24. Now on the way the Blessed One went aside from the highway and stopped at the foot of a tree. And he said to the Venerable Ānanda: "Please fold my upper robe in four, Ānanda, and lay it down. I am weary and want to rest awhile."

"So be it, Lord." And the Venerable Ānanda folded the robe in four and laid it down.

25. And the Blessed One sat down on the seat prepared for him and said to the Venerable Ānanda: "Please bring me some water, Ānanda. I am thirsty and want to drink."

26. And the Venerable Ānanda answered the Blessed One: "But just now, Lord, a great number of carts, five hundred carts, have passed over, and the shallow water has been cut through by the wheels, so that it flows turbid and muddy. But the Kakutthā River, Lord, is quite close by, and its waters are clear, pleasant, cool, and translucent. It is easily approachable and delightfully placed. There the Blessed One can quench his thirst and refresh his limbs."

27–29. But a second time the Blessed One made his request, and the Venerable Ānanda answered him as before. And then for a third time the Blessed One said: "Please bring me some water, Ānanda. I am thirsty and want to drink."

30. Then the Venerable Ānanda answered, saying: "So be it, Lord." And he took the bowl and went to the stream. And the shallow water, which had been cut through by the wheels so that it flowed turbid and muddy, became clear and settled down, pure and pleasant as the Venerable Ānanda drew near.

31. Then the Venerable Ānanda thought: "Marvellous and most wonderful indeed is the power and glory of the Tathāgata!"

32. And he took up water in the bowl and carried it to the Blessed One, and said: "Marvellous and most wonderful indeed is the power and glory of the Tathāgata! For this shallow water, which had been cut through by the wheels so that it flowed turbid and muddy, became clear and settled down, pure and pleasant as I drew near. Now let the Blessed

One drink the water. Let the Happy One drink." And the Blessed One drank the water.

Pukkusa the Malla

33. Now it so happened that one Pukkusa of the Malla clan, who was a disciple of Āḷāra Kālāma, was passing by on his way from Kusinārā to Pāvā.[40]

34. And when he saw the Blessed One seated at the foot of a tree, he approached him, respectfully greeted him, and sat down at one side. And he spoke to the Blessed One, saying: "Marvellous it is, Lord, most wonderful it is, O Lord, the state of calmness wherein abide those who have gone forth from the world.

35. "For at one time, Lord, Āḷāra Kālāma was on a journey, and he went aside from the highway and sat down by the wayside at the foot of a tree to pass the heat of the day. And it came about, Lord, that a great number of carts, even five hundred carts, passed by him, one by one. And then, Lord, a certain man who was following behind that train of carts, approached and spoke to him, saying: 'Did you, sir, see a great number of carts that passed you by?' And Āḷāra Kālāma answered him: 'I did not see them, brother.' 'But the noise, sir, surely you heard?' 'I did not hear it, brother.' Then that man asked him: 'Then, sir, perhaps you slept?' 'No, brother, I was not sleeping.' 'Then, sir, were you conscious?' 'I was, brother.' Then that man said: 'Then, sir, while conscious and awake you still did not see the great number of carts, even five hundred carts, that passed you by one after another, nor heard the noise? Why, sir, your very robe is covered with their dust!' And Āḷāra Kālāma replied, saying: 'So it is, brother.'

36. "And to that man, O Lord, came the thought: 'Mar-

vellous it is, most wonderful indeed it is, the state of calmness wherein abide those who have gone forth from the world!' And there arose in him great faith in Āḷāra Kālāma, and he went his way."

37. "Now what do you think, Pukkusa? What is more difficult to do, more difficult to meet with—that a man, while conscious and awake, should not see a great number of carts, even five hundred carts, that passed him by one after another, nor hear the noise, or that one conscious and awake, in the midst of a heavy rain, with thunder rolling, lightning flashing, and thunderbolts crashing, should neither see it nor hear the noise?"

38. "What, O Lord, are five hundred carts—nay, six, seven, eight, nine hundred, or a thousand or even hundreds of thousands of carts—compared with this?"

39. "Now one time, Pukkusa, I was staying at Ātumā, and had my abode in a barn there. And at that time there was a heavy rain, with thunder rolling, lightning flashing, and thunderbolts crashing. And two farmers who were brothers were killed close to the barn, together with four oxen, and a great crowd came forth from Ātumā to the spot where they were killed.

40. "Now at that time, Pukkusa, I had come out of the barn and was walking up and down in thought before the door. And a certain man from the great crowd approached me, respectfully greeted me, and stood at one side.

41. "And I asked him: 'Why, brother, has this great crowd gathered together?' And he answered me: 'Just now, Lord, there was a heavy rain, with thunder rolling, lightning flashing, and thunderbolts crashing. And two farmers who were brothers were killed close by, together with four oxen. It is because of this that the great crowd has gathered. But where, Lord, were you?'

" 'I was here, brother.' 'Yet, Lord, did you not see it?' 'I did not see it, brother.' 'But the noise, Lord, you surely heard?' 'I did not hear it, brother.' Then that man asked me: 'Then, Lord, perhaps you slept?' 'No, brother, I was not sleeping.' 'Then, Lord, you were conscious?' 'I was, brother.' Then that man said: 'Then, Lord, while conscious and awake, in the midst of a heavy rain, with thunder rolling, lightning flashing, and thunderbolts crashing, you neither saw it nor heard the noise?' And I answered him, saying: 'I did not, brother.'

42. "And to that man, Pukkusa, came the thought: 'Marvellous it is, most wonderful indeed it is, the state of calmness wherein abide those who have gone forth from the world!' And there arose in him great faith in me, and he respectfully saluted me, and keeping his right side towards me, he went his way."

43. When this had been said, Pukkusa of the Malla clan said to the Blessed One: "The faith, Lord, that I had in Āḷāra Kālāma I now scatter to the mighty wind, I let it be carried away as by a flowing stream! Excellent, O Lord, most excellent, O Lord! It is as if, Lord, one were to set upright what had been overthrown, or to reveal what had been hidden, or to show the path to one who had gone astray, or to light a lamp in the darkness so that those having eyes might see—even so has the Blessed One set forth the Dhamma in many ways. And so, O Lord, I take my refuge in the Blessed One, the Dhamma, and the Community of Bhikkhus. May the Blessed One accept me as his disciple, one who has taken refuge until the end of life."

44. Then Pukkusa of the Malla clan spoke to a certain man, saying: "Bring me at once, friend, two sets of golden-hued robes, burnished and ready for wear." And the man answered him: "So be it, sir."

45. And when the robes were brought, Pukkusa of the Malla clan offered them to the Blessed One, saying: "May the Blessed One, O Lord, out of compassion, accept this from me." And the Blessed One said: "Robe me, then in one, Pukkusa, and in the other robe Ānanda."

"So be it, Lord." And he thereupon robed the Blessed One in one, and in the other he robed the Venerable Ānanda.

46. And then the Blessed One instructed Pukkusa of the Malla clan in the Dhamma, and roused, edified, and gladdened him. And after that, Pukkusa rose from his seat, respectfully saluted the Blessed One, and keeping his right side towards him, went his way.

47. And soon after Pukkusa of the Malla clan had departed, the Venerable Ānanda arranged the set of golden-hued robes, burnished and ready for wear, about the body of the Blessed One. But when the set of robes was arranged upon the body of the Blessed One, it became as though faded, and its splendour dimmed.

48. And the Venerable Ānanda said to the Blessed One: "Marvellous it is, O Lord, most wonderful indeed it is, how clear and radiant the skin of the Tathāgata appears! This set of golden-hued robes, burnished and ready for wear, Lord, now that it is arranged upon the body of the Blessed One seems to have become faded, its splendour dimmed."

49. "It is so, Ānanda. There are two occasions, Ānanda, when the skin of the Tathāgata appears exceedingly clear and radiant. Which are these two? The night, Ānanda, when the Tathāgata becomes fully enlightened in unsurpassed, supreme Enlightenment, and the night when the Tathāgata comes to his final passing away into the state of Nibbāna in which no element of clinging remains. These, Ānanda, are the two occasions on which the skin of the Tathāgata appears exceedingly clear and radiant.

50. "And now today, in the last watch of this very night, Ānanda, in the Mallas' Sāla Grove, in the vicinity of Kusinārā, between two sāla trees, the Tathāgata will come to his Parinibbāna. So now, Ānanda, let us go to the Kakutthā River."

51. Clad in Pukkusa's gift, the robes of gold,
The Master's form was radiant to behold.

At the Kakutthā River

52. Then the Blessed One went to the Kakutthā River together with a great community of bhikkhus.

53. And he went down into the water and bathed and drank. And coming forth from the water again, he went to the Mango Grove, and there spoke to the Venerable Cundaka, saying: "Please fold my upper robe in four, Cundaka, and lay it down. I am weary and would rest awhile."

"So be it, Lord." And Cundaka folded the robe in four and laid it down.

54. And the Blessed One lay down on his right side, in the lion's posture, resting one foot upon the other, and so disposed himself, mindfully and clearly comprehending, with the time for rising held in mind. And the Venerable Cundaka sat down right in front of the Blessed One.

55. The Buddha to Kakutthā's river came,
Where cool and limpid flows the pleasant stream;
There washed in water clear his weary frame
The Buddha—he in all the world supreme!
And having bathed and drank, the Teacher straight
Crossed over, the bhikkhus thronging in his wake.

Discoursing holy truths, the Master great
Towards the Mango Grove his path did take.

There to the elder Cundaka he spoke:
"Lay down my robe, please, folded into four."
Then the elder, swift as lightning stroke,
Hastened the Teacher's bidding to obey.
Weary, the Lord then lay down on the mat,
And Cunda on the ground before him sat.

Relieving Cunda's Remorse

56. Then the Blessed One spoke to the Venerable Ānanda, saying: "It may come to pass, Ānanda, that someone will cause remorse to Cunda the metalworker, saying: 'It is no gain to you, friend Cunda, but a loss, that it was from you the Tathāgata took his last alms meal, and then came to his end.' Then, Ānanda, the remorse of Cunda should be dispelled after this manner: 'It is a gain to you, friend Cunda, a blessing that the Tathāgata took his last alms meal from you, and then came to his end. For, friend, face to face with the Blessed One I have heard and learned: "There are two offerings of food which are of equal fruition, of equal outcome, exceeding in grandeur the fruition and result of any other offerings of food. Which two? The one partaken of by the Tathāgata before becoming fully enlightened in unsurpassed, supreme Enlightenment; and the one partaken of by the Tathāgata before passing into the state of Nibbāna in which no element of clinging remains. By his deed the worthy Cunda has accumulated merit which makes for long life, beauty, well being, glory, heavenly rebirth, and sovereignty." ' Thus, Ānanda, the remorse of Cunda the metalworker should be dispelled."

57. Then the Blessed One, understanding that matter, breathed forth the solemn utterance:

Who gives, his virtues shall increase;
Who is self-curbed, no hatred bears;
Whoso is skilled in virtue, evil shuns,
And by the rooting out of lust and hate
And all delusion, comes to be at peace."

PART FIVE

At Kusinārā

Last Place of Rest

1. Then the Blessed One addressed the Venerable Ānanda, saying: "Come, Ānanda, let us cross to the farther bank of the Hiraññavatī, and go to the Mallas' Sāla Grove, in the vicinity of Kusinārā."

"So be it, Lord."

2. And the Blessed One, together with a large company of bhikkhus, went to the further bank of the river Hiraññavatī, to the Sāla Grove of the Mallas, in the vicinity of Kusinārā. And there he spoke to the Venerable Ānanda, saying:

3. "Please, Ānanda, prepare for me a couch between the twin sāla trees, with the head to the north. I am weary, Ānanda, and want to lie down."[41]

"So be it, Lord." And the Venerable Ānanda did as the Blessed One asked him to do.

Then the Blessed One lay down on his right side, in the lion's posture, resting one foot upon the other, and so disposed himself, mindfully and clearly comprehending.

4. At that time the twin sāla trees broke out in full bloom, though it was not the season of flowering. And the blossoms rained upon the body of the Tathāgata and dropped and scattered and were strewn upon it in worship of the Tathāgata. And celestial *mandārava* flowers and heavenly sandalwood powder from the sky rained down upon the body of the

Tathāgata, and dropped and scattered and were strewn upon it in worship of the Tathāgata. And the sound of heavenly voices and heavenly instruments made music in the air out of reverence for the Tathāgata.

5. And the Blessed One spoke to the Venerable Ānanda, saying: "Ānanda, the twin sāla trees are in full bloom, though it is not the season of flowering. And the blossoms rain upon the body of the Tathāgata and drop and scatter and are strewn upon it in worship of the Tathāgata. And celestial coral flowers and heavenly sandalwood powder from the sky rain down upon the body of the Tathāgata, and drop and scatter and are strewn upon it in worship of the Tathāgata. And the sound of heavenly voices and heavenly instruments makes music in the air out of reverence for the Tathāgata.

6. "Yet it is not thus, Ānanda, that the Tathāgata is respected, venerated, esteemed, worshipped, and honoured in the highest degree. But, Ānanda, whatever bhikkhu or bhikkhunī, layman or laywoman, abides by the Dhamma, lives uprightly in the Dhamma, walks in the way of the Dhamma, it is by such a one that the Tathāgata is respected, venerated, esteemed, worshipped, and honoured in the highest degree. Therefore, Ānanda, thus should you train yourselves: 'We shall abide by the Dhamma, live uprightly in the Dhamma, walk in the way of the Dhamma.' "

The Grief of the Gods

7. At that time the Venerable Upavāṇa was standing before the Blessed One, fanning him. And the Blessed One rebuked him, saying: "Move aside, bhikkhu, do not stand in front of me."

8. And to the Venerable Ānanda came the thought: "This Venerable Upavāṇa has been in attendance on the Blessed

One for a long time, closely associating with him and serving him. Yet now, right at the end, the Blessed One rebukes him. What now could be the reason, what the cause for the Blessed One to rebuke the Venerable Upavāṇa, saying: 'Move aside, bhikkhu, do not stand in front of me'?"

9–10. And the Venerable Ānanda told his thought to the Blessed One. The Blessed One said: "Throughout the tenfold world-system, Ānanda, there are hardly any of the deities that have not gathered together to look upon the Tathāgata. For a distance of twelve yojanas around the Sāla Grove of the Mallas in the vicinity of Kusinārā there is not a spot that could be pricked with the tip of a hair that is not filled with powerful deities. And these deities, Ānanda, are complaining: 'From afar have we come to look upon the Tathāgata. For rare in the world is the arising of Tathāgatas, Arahats, Fully Enlightened Ones. And this day, in the last watch of the night, the Tathāgata's Parinibbāna will come about. But this bhikkhu of great powers has placed himself right in front of the Blessed One, concealing him, so that now, at the very end, we are prevented from looking upon him.' Thus, Ānanda, the deities complain."

11. "Of what kind of deities, Lord, is the Blessed One aware?"

12–13. "There are deities, Ānanda, in space and on earth, who are earthly-minded; with dishevelled hair they weep, with uplifted arms they weep; flinging themselves on the ground, they roll from side to side, lamenting: 'Too soon has the Blessed One come to his Parinibbāna! Too soon has the Happy One come to his Parinibbāna! Too soon will the Eye of the World vanish from sight!'

14. "But those deities who are freed from passion, mindful and comprehending, reflect in this way: 'Impermanent are all compounded things. How could this be otherwise?' "

Ānanda's Concern

15. "Formerly, Lord, on leaving their quarters after the rains, the bhikkhus would set forth to see the Tathāgata, and to us there was the gain and benefit of receiving and associating with those very revered bhikkhus who came to have audience with the Blessed One and to wait upon him. But, Lord, after the Blessed One has gone, we shall no longer have that gain and benefit."

Four Places of Pilgrimage

16. "There are four places, Ānanda, that a pious person should visit and look upon with feelings of reverence.[42] What are the four?

17. " 'Here the Tathāgata was born!'[43] This, Ānanda, is a place that a pious person should visit and look upon with feelings of reverence.

18. " 'Here the Tathāgata became fully enlightened in unsurpassed, supreme Enlightenment!'[44] This, Ānanda, is a place that a pious person should visit and look upon with feelings of reverence.

19. " 'Here the Tathāgata set rolling the unexcelled Wheel of the Dhamma!'[45] This, Ānanda, is a place that a pious person should visit and look upon with feelings of reverence.

20. " 'Here the Tathāgata passed away into the state of Nibbāna in which no element of clinging remains!' This, Ānanda, is a place that a pious person should visit and look upon with feelings of reverence.

21. "These, Ānanda, are the four places that a pious person should visit and look upon with feelings of reverence. And truly there will come to these places, Ānanda, pious bhikkhus and bhikkhunis, laymen and laywomen, reflecting: 'Here the Tathāgata was born! Here the Tathāgata became

fully enlightened in unsurpassed, supreme Enlightenment! Here the Tathāgata set rolling the unexcelled Wheel of the Dhamma! Here the Tathāgata passed away into the state of Nibbāna in which no element of clinging remains!'

22. "And whoever, Ānanda, should die on such a pilgrimage with his heart established in faith, at the breaking up of the body, after death, will be reborn in a realm of heavenly happiness."

23. Then the Venerable Ānanda said to the Blessed One: "How, Lord, should we conduct ourselves towards women?"

"Do not see them, Ānanda."

"But, Lord, if we do see them?"

"Do not speak, Ānanda."

"But, Lord, if they should speak to us?"

"Then, Ānanda, you should establish mindfulness."

24. Then the Venerable Ānanda said: "How should we act, Lord, respecting the body of the Tathāgata?"

"Do not hinder yourselves, Ānanda, to honour the body of the Tathāgata. Rather you should strive, Ānanda, and be zealous on your own behalf,[46] for your own good. Unflinchingly, ardently, and resolutely you should apply yourselves to your own good. For there are, Ānanda, wise nobles, wise brahmins, and wise householders who are devoted to the Tathāgata, and it is they who will render the honour to the body of the Tathāgata."

25. Then the Venerable Ānanda said: "But how, Lord, should they act respecting the body of the Tathāgata?"

"After the same manner, Ānanda, as towards the body of a universal monarch."[47]

"But how, Lord, do they act respecting the body of a universal monarch?"

26. "The body of a universal monarch, Ānanda, is first wrapped round with new linen, and then with teased cotton

wool, and so it is done up to five hundred layers of linen and five hundred of cotton wool. When that is done, the body of the universal monarch is placed in an iron[48] oil vessel, which is enclosed in another iron vessel, a funeral pyre is built of all kinds of perfumed woods, and so the body of the universal monarch is burned; and at a crossroads a stūpa is raised for the universal monarch. So it is done, Ānanda, with the body of a universal monarch. And even, Ānanda, as with the body of a universal monarch, so should it be done with the body of the Tathāgata; and at a crossroads also a stūpa should be raised for the Tathāgata. And whosoever shall bring to that place garlands or incense or sandalpaste, or pay reverence, and whose mind becomes calm there—it will be to his well being and happiness for a long time.

27. "There are four persons, Ānanda, who are worthy of a stūpa. Who are those four? A Tathāgata, an Arahat, a Fully Enlightened One is worthy of a stūpa; so also is a Paccekabuddha,[49] and a disciple of a Tathāgata, and a universal monarch.

28–31. "And why, Ānanda, is a Tathāgata, an Arahat, a Fully Enlightened One worthy of a stūpa? Because, Ānanda, at the thought: 'This is the stūpa of that Blessed One, Arahat, Fully Enlightened One!' the hearts of many people will be calmed and made happy; and so calmed and with their minds established in faith therein, at the breaking up of the body, after death, they will be reborn in a realm of heavenly happiness. And so also at the thought: 'This is the stūpa of that Paccekabuddha!' or 'This is the stūpa of a disciple of that Tathāgata, Arahat, Fully Enlightened One!' or 'This is the stūpa of that righteous monarch who ruled according to Dhamma!'—the hearts of many people are calmed and made happy; and so calmed and with their minds established in faith therein, at the breaking up of the body, after death, they will be reborn in a realm of heavenly happiness. And it is because of this, Ānanda, that these four persons are worthy of a stūpa."

Ānanda's Grief

32. Then the Venerable Ānanda went into the vihāra[50] and leaned against the doorpost and wept: "I am still but a learner,[51] and still have to strive for my own perfection. But, alas, my Master, who was so compassionate towards me, is about to pass away!"

33. And the Blessed One spoke to the bhikkhus, saying: "Where, bhikkhus, is Ānanda?"

"The Venerable Ānanda, Lord, has gone into the vihāra and there stands leaning against the door post and weeping: 'I am still but a learner, and still have to strive for my own perfection. But, alas, my Master, who was so compassionate towards me, is about to pass away!' "

34. Then the Blessed One asked a certain bhikkhu to bring the Venerable Ānanda to him, saying: "Go, bhikkhu, and say to Ānanda, 'Friend Ānanda, the Master calls you.' "

"So be it, Lord." And that bhikkhu went and spoke to the Venerable Ānanda as the Blessed One had asked him to. And the Venerable Ānanda went to the Blessed One, bowed down to him, and sat down on one side.

35. Then the Blessed One spoke to the Venerable Ānanda, saying: "Enough, Ānanda! Do not grieve, do not lament! For have I not taught from the very beginning that with all that is dear and beloved there must be change, separation, and severence? Of that which is born, come into being, compounded, and subject to decay, how can one say: 'May it not come to dissolution!'? There can be no such state of things. Now for a long time, Ānanda, you have served the Tathāgata

with loving-kindness in deed, word, and thought, graciously, pleasantly, with a whole heart and beyond measure. Great good have you gathered, Ānanda! Now you should put forth energy, and soon you too will be free from the taints."[52]

Praise of Ānanda

36. Then the Blessed One addressed the bhikkhus, saying: "Bhikkhus, the Blessed Ones, Arahats, Fully Enlightened Ones of times past also had excellent and devoted attendant bhikkhus, such as I have in Ānanda. And so also, bhikkhus, will the Blessed Ones, Arahats, Fully Enlightened Ones of times to come.

37. "Capable and judicious is Ānanda, bhikkhus, for he knows the proper time for bhikkhus to have audience with the Tathāgata, and the time for bhikkhunīs, the time for laymen and for laywomen; the time for kings and for ministers of state; the time for teachers of other sects and for their followers.

38. "In Ānanda, bhikkhus, are to be found four rare and superlative qualities. What are the four? If, bhikkhus, a company of bhikkhus should go to see Ānanda, they become joyful on seeing him; and if he then speaks to them of the Dhamma, they are made joyful by his discourse; and when he becomes silent, they are disappointed. So it is also when bhikkhunīs, laymen, or laywomen go to see Ānanda: they become joyful on seeing him; and if he then speaks to them of the Dhamma, they are made joyful by his discourse; and when he becomes silent, they are disappointed.

39. "In a universal monarch, bhikkhus, are to be found four rare and superlative qualities. What are those four? If, bhikkhus, a company of nobles should go to see the universal monarch, they become joyful on seeing him; and if he

then speaks, they are made joyful by his talk; and when he becomes silent, they are disappointed. So it is also when a company of brahmins, of householders, or of ascetics goes to see a universal monarch.

40. "And in just the same way, bhikkhus, in Ānanda are to be found these four rare and superlative qualities."

The Past Glory of Kusinārā

41. When this had been said, the Venerable Ānanda spoke to the Blessed One, saying: "Let it not be, Lord, that the Blessed One should pass away in this mean place, this uncivilized township in the midst of the jungle, a mere outpost of the province. There are great cities, Lord, such as Campā, Rājagaha, Sāvatthī, Sāketa, Kosambī, and Benares—let the Blessed One have his final passing away in one of those. For in those cities dwell many wealthy nobles and brahmins and householders who are devotees of the Tathāgata, and they will render due honour to the remains of the Tathāgata."

42. "Do not say that, Ānanda! Do not say: 'This mean place, this uncivilized township in the midst of the jungle, a mere outpost of the province.' In times long past, Ānanda, there was a king by the name of Mahā Sudassana, who was a universal monarch, a king of righteousness, a conqueror of the four quarters of the earth, whose realm was established in security, and who was endowed with the seven jewels.[53] And that King Mahā Sudassana, Ānanda, had his royal residence here at Kusinārā, which was then called Kusāvatī, and it extended twelve yojanas from east to west, and seven from north to south.

43. "And mighty, Ānanda, was Kusāvatī, the capital, prosperous and well populated, much frequented by people, and abundantly provided with food. Just as the royal residence

of the deities, Āḷakamandā, is mighty, prosperous, and well populated, much frequented by deities and abundantly provided with food, so was the royal capital of Kusāvatī.

44. "Kusāvatī, Ānanda, resounded unceasingly day and night with ten sounds—the trumpeting of elephants, the neighing of horses, the rattling of chariots, the beating of drums and tabours, music and song, cheers, the clapping of hands, and cries of 'Eat, drink, and be merry!'

Lamentation of the Mallas

45. "Go now, Ānanda, to Kusinārā and announce to the Mallas: 'Today, Vāseṭṭhas, in the last watch of the night, the Tathāgata's Parinibbāna will take place. Approach, O Vāseṭṭhas, draw near! Do not be remorseful later at the thought: "In our township it was that the Tathāgata's Parinibbāna took place, but we failed to see him at the end!" '"

"So be it, Lord." And the Venerable Ānanda prepared himself, and taking bowl and robe, went with a companion to Kusinārā.

46. Now at that time the Mallas had gathered in the council hall for some public business. And the Venerable Ānanda approached them and announced: "Today, Vāseṭṭhas, in the last watch of the night, the Tathāgata's Parinibbāna will take place. Approach, Vāseṭṭhas, draw near! Do not be remorseful later at the thought: 'In our township it was that the Tathāgata's Parinibbāna took place, but we failed to see him at the end.' "

47. When they heard the Venerable Ānanda speak these words, the Mallas with their sons, their wives, and the wives of their sons, were sorely grieved, grieved at heart and afflicted; and some, with their hair all dishevelled, with arms uplifted in despair, wept; flinging themselves on the ground,

they rolled from side to side, lamenting: "Too soon has the Blessed One come to his Parinibbāna! Too soon has the Happy One come to his Parinibbāna! Too soon will the Eye of the World vanish from sight!"

48. And thus afflicted and filled with grief, the Mallas, with their sons, their wives, and the wives of their sons, went to the Sāla Grove, the recreation park of the Mallas, to the place where the Venerable Ānanda was.

49. And the thought arose in the Venerable Ānanda: "If I were to allow the Mallas of Kusinārā to pay reverence to the Blessed One one by one, the night will have given place to dawn before they are all presented to him. Therefore let me divide them up according to clan, each family in a group, and so present them to the Blessed One thus: 'The Malla of such and such a name, Lord, with his wives and children, his attendants and his friends, pays homage at the feet of the Blessed One.' "

50. And the Venerable Ānanda divided the Mallas up according to clan, each family in a group, and presented them to the Blessed One. So it was that the Venerable Ānanda caused the Mallas of Kusinārā to be presented to the Blessed One by clans, each family in a group, even in the first watch of the night.

The Last Convert

51. Now at that time a wandering ascetic named Subhadda was dwelling at Kusinārā. And Subhadda the wandering ascetic heard it said: "Today in the third watch of the night, the Parinibbāna of the ascetic Gotama will take place."

52. And the thought arose in him: "I have heard it said by old and venerable wandering ascetics, teachers of teachers, that the arising of Tathāgatas, Arahats, Fully Enlightened

Ones, is rare in the world. Yet this very day, in the last watch of the night, the Parinibbāna of the ascetic Gotama will take place. Now there is in me a doubt; but to this extent I have faith in the ascetic Gotama, that he could so teach me the Dhamma as to remove that doubt."

53. Then the wandering ascetic Subhadda went to the Sāla Grove, the recreation park of the Mallas, and drew near to the Venerable Ānanda, and told the Venerable Ānanda his thought. And he spoke to the Venerable Ānanda, saying: "Friend Ānanda, it would be good if I could be allowed into the presence of the ascetic Gotama."

54. But the Venerable Ānanda answered him, saying: "Enough, friend Subhadda! Do not trouble the Tathāgata. The Blessed One is weary."

55–56. Yet a second and a third time the wandering ascetic Subhadda made his request, and a second and a third time the Venerable Ānanda refused him.

57. And the Blessed One heard the talk between them, and he called the Venerable Ānanda and said: "Stop, Ānanda! Do not refuse Subhadda. Subhadda, Ānanda, may be allowed into the presence of the Tathāgata. For whatever he will ask me, he will ask for the sake of knowledge, and not as an offence. And the answer I give him, that he will readily understand."

58. Thereupon the Venerable Ānanda said to the wandering ascetic Subhadda: "Go then, friend Subhadda, the Blessed One gives you leave."

59. Then the wandering ascetic Subhadda approached the Blessed One and saluted him courteously. And having exchanged with him pleasant and civil greetings, the wandering ascetic Subhadda seated himself at one side and addressed

the Blessed One, saying: "There are, Venerable Gotama, ascetics and brahmins who are heads of great companies of disciples, who have large retinues, who are leaders of schools, well known and renowned, and held in high esteem by the multitude, such teachers as Pūraṇa Kassapa, Makkhali Gosāla, Ajita Kesakambalī, Pakudha Kaccāyana, Sañjaya Belaṭṭhiputta, Nigaṇṭha Nātaputta. Have all of these attained realization, as each of them would have it believed, or has none of them, or is it that some have attained realization and others not?"

60. "Enough, Subhadda! Let it be as it may, whether all of them have attained realization, as each of them would have it believed, or whether none of them has, or whether some have attained realization and others not. I will teach you the Dhamma, Subhadda; listen and heed it well, and I will speak."

"So be it, Lord."

The Lion's Roar

61. And the Blessed One spoke, saying: "In whatsoever Dhamma and Discipline, Subhadda, there is not found the Noble Eightfold Path, neither is there found a true ascetic of the first, second, third, or fourth degree of saintliness. But in whatsoever Dhamma and Discipline there is found the Noble Eightfold Path, there is found a true ascetic of the first, second, third, and fourth degrees of saintliness.[54] Now in this Dhamma and Discipline, Subhadda, is found the Noble Eightfold Path; and in it alone are also found true ascetics of the first, second, third, and fourth degrees of saintliness. Devoid of true ascetics are the systems of other teachers. But if, Subhadda, the bhikkhus live righteously, the world will not be destitute of arahats.

62. "In age but twenty-nine was I, Subhadda,
When I renounced the world to seek the Good;
Fifty-one years have passed since then, Subhadda,
And in all that time a wanderer have I been
In the domain of virtue and of truth,
And except therein, there is no saint
(of the first degree).

"And there is none of the second degree, nor of the third degree, nor of the fourth degree of saintliness. Devoid of true ascetics are the systems of other teachers. But if, Subhadda, the bhikkhus live righteously, the world will not be destitute of arahats."

63. When this was said, the wandering ascetic Subhadda spoke to the Blessed One, saying: "Excellent, O Lord, most excellent, O Lord! It is as if, Lord, one were to set upright what had been overthrown, or to reveal what had been hidden, or to show the path to one who had gone astray, or to light a lamp in the darkness so that those with eyes might see—even so has the Blessed One set forth the Dhamma in many ways. And so, O Lord, I take my refuge in the Blessed One, the Dhamma, and the Community of Bhikkhus. May I receive from the Blessed One admission to the Order and also the higher ordination."

64. "Whoever, Subhadda, having been formerly a follower of another creed, wishes to receive admission and higher ordination in this Dhamma and Discipline, remains on probation for a period of four months. At the end of those four months, if the bhikkhus are satisfied with him, they grant him admission and higher ordination as a bhikkhu. Yet in this matter I recognize differences of personalities."

65. "If, O Lord, whoever, having been formerly a follower of another creed, wishes to receive admission and higher ordination in this Dhamma and Discipline, remains on probation for a period of four months, and at the end of those four months, if the bhikkhus are satisfied with him, they grant him admission and higher ordination as a bhikkhu—then I will remain on probation for a period of four years. And at the end of those four years, if the bhikkhus are satisfied with me, let them grant me admission and higher ordination as a bhikkhu."

66. But the Blessed One called the Venerable Ānanda and said to him: "Ānanda, let Subhadda be given admission into the Order." And the Venerable Ānanda replied: "So be it, Lord."

67. Then the wandering ascetic Subhadda said to the Venerable Ānanda: "It is a gain to you, friend Ānanda, a blessing, that in the presence of the Master himself you have received the sprinkling of ordination as a disciple."

68. So it came about that the wandering ascetic Subhadda, in the presence of the Blessed One, received admission and higher ordination. And from the time of his ordination the Venerable Subhadda remained alone, secluded, heedful, ardent, and resolute. And before long he attained to the goal for which a worthy man goes forth rightly from home to homelessness, the supreme goal of the holy life; and having by himself realized it with higher knowledge, he dwelt therein. He knew: "Destroyed is birth; the higher life is fulfilled; nothing more is to be done, and beyond this life nothing more remains." And the Venerable Subhadda became yet another among the arahats, and he was the last disciple converted by the Blessed One himself.

Part Six
The Passing Away

The Blessed One's Final Exhortation

1. Now the Blessed One spoke to the Venerable Ānanda, saying: "It may be, Ānanda, that to some among you the thought will come: 'Ended is the word of the Master; we have a Master no longer.' But it should not, Ānanda, be so considered. For that which I have proclaimed and made known as the Dhamma and the Discipline, that shall be your Master when I am gone.

2. "And, Ānanda, whereas now the bhikkhus address one another as 'friend,' let it not be so when I am gone. The senior bhikkhus, Ānanda, may address the junior ones by their name, their family name, or as 'friend'; but the junior bhikkhus should address the senior ones as 'venerable sir' or 'your reverence.'[55]

3. "If it is desired, Ānanda, the Sangha may, when I am gone, abolish the lesser and minor rules.[56]

4. "Ānanda, when I am gone, let the higher penalty be imposed upon the bhikkhu Channa."[57]

"But what, Lord, is the higher penalty?"

"The bhikkhu Channa, Ānanda, may say what he will, but the bhikkhus should neither converse with him, nor exhort him, nor admonish him."

5. Then the Blessed One addressed the bhikkhus, saying: "It may be, bhikkhus, that one of you is in doubt or perplex-

ity as to the Buddha, the Dhamma, or the Sangha, the path or the practice. Then question, bhikkhus! Do not be given to remorse later on with the thought: 'The Master was with us face to face, yet face to face we failed to ask him.' "

6. But when this was said, the bhikkhus were silent. And yet a second and a third time the Blessed One said to them: "It may be, bhikkhus, that one of you is in doubt or perplexity as to the Buddha, the Dhamma, or the Sangha, the path or the practice. Then question, bhikkhus! Do not be given to remorse later on with the thought: 'The Master was with us face to face, yet face to face we failed to ask him.' "

And for a second and a third time the bhikkhus were silent. Then the Blessed One said to them: "It may be, bhikkhus, out of respect for the Master that you ask no questions. Then, bhikkhus, let friend communicate it to friend." Yet still the bhikkhus were silent.

7. And the Venerable Ānanda spoke to the Blessed One, saying: "Marvellous it is, O Lord, most wonderful it is! This faith I have in the community of bhikkhus, that not even one bhikkhu is in doubt or perplexity as to the Buddha, the Dhamma, or the Sangha, the path or the practice."

"Out of faith, Ānanda, you speak thus. But here, Ānanda, the Tathāgata knows for certain that among this community of bhikkhus there is not even one bhikkhu who is in doubt or perplexity as to the Buddha, the Dhamma, or the Sangha, the path or the practice. For, Ānanda, among these five hundred bhikkhus even the lowest is a stream-enterer, secure from downfall, assured, and bound for enlightenment."

8. And the Blessed One addressed the bhikkhus, saying: "Behold now, bhikkhus, I exhort you: All compounded things are subject to vanish. Strive with earnestness!"[58]

This was the last word of the Tathāgata.

How the Blessed One Passed into Nibbāna

9. And the Blessed One entered the first jhāna. Rising from the first jhāna, he entered the second jhāna. Rising from the second jhāna, he entered the third jhāna. Rising from the third jhāna, he entered the fourth jhāna. And rising out of the fourth jhāna, he entered the sphere of infinite space. Rising from the attainment of the sphere of infinite space, he entered the sphere of infinite consciousness. Rising from the attainment of the sphere of infinite consciousness, he entered the sphere of nothingness. Rising from the attainment of the sphere of nothingness, he entered the sphere of neither-perception-nor-non-perception. And rising out of the attainment of the sphere of neither-perception-nor-non-perception, he attained to the cessation of perception and feeling.

10. And the Venerable Ānanda spoke to the Venerable Anuruddha, saying: "Venerable Anuruddha, the Blessed One has passed away."

"No, friend Ānanda, the Blessed One has not passed away. He has entered the state of the cessation of perception and feeling."[59]

11. Then the Blessed One, rising from the cessation of perception and feeling, entered the sphere of neither-perception-nor-non-perception. Rising from the attainment of the sphere of neither-perception-nor-non-perception, he entered the sphere of nothingness. Rising from the attainment of the sphere of nothingness, he entered the sphere of infinite consciousness. Rising from the attainment of the sphere of infinite consciousness, he entered the sphere of infinite space. Rising from the attainment of the sphere of infinite space, he entered the fourth jhāna. Rising from the fourth jhāna, he entered the third jhāna. Rising from the third jhāna, he entered the second jhāna. Rising from the second jhāna, he entered the first jhāna.

Rising from the first jhāna, he entered the second jhāna. Rising from the second jhāna, he entered the third jhāna. Rising from the third jhāna, he entered the fourth jhāna. And, rising from the fourth jhāna, the Blessed One immediately passed away.

The World's Echo

12. And when the Blessed One had passed away, simultaneously with his Parinibbāna there came a tremendous earthquake, dreadful and astounding, and the thunders rolled across the heavens.

13. And when the Blessed One had passed away, simultaneously with his Parinibbāna, Brahmā Sahampati[60] spoke this stanza:

"All must depart—all beings that have life
Must shed their compound forms. Yea, even one,
A Master such as he, a peerless being,
Powerful in wisdom, the Enlightened One, has passed away."

14. And when the Blessed One had passed away, simultaneously with his Parinibbāna, Sakka, king of the gods,[61] spoke this stanza:

"Transient are all compounded things,
Subject to arise and vanish;
Having come into existence they pass away;
Good is the peace when they forever cease."

15. And when the Blessed One had passed away, simultaneously with his Parinibbāna, the Venerable Anuruddha spoke this stanza:

"No movement of the breath, but with steadfast heart,
Free from desires and tranquil—so the sage
Comes to his end. By mortal pangs unshaken,
His mind, like a flame extinguished, finds release."

16. And when the Blessed One had passed away, simultaneously with his Parinibbāna, the Venerable Ānanda spoke this stanza:

"Then there was terror, and the hair stood up, when he,
The All-accomplished One, the Buddha, passed away."

17. Then, when the Blessed One had passed away, some bhikkhus, not yet freed from passion, lifted up their arms and wept; and some, flinging themselves on the ground, rolled from side to side and wept, lamenting: "Too soon has the Blessed One come to his Parinibbāna! Too soon has the Happy One come to his Parinibbāna! Too soon has the Eye of the World vanished from sight!"

But the bhikkhus who were freed from passion, mindful and clearly comprehending, reflected in this way: "Impermanent are all compounded things. How could this be otherwise?"

18. And the Venerable Anuruddha addressed the bhikkhus, saying: "Enough, friends! Do not grieve, do not lament! For has not the Blessed One declared that with all that is dear and beloved there must be change, separation, and severance? Of that which is born, come into being, compounded and subject to decay, how can one say: 'May it not come to dissolution!'? The deities, friends, are aggrieved."

"But, venerable sir, of what deities is the Venerable Anuruddha aware?"

"There are deities, friend Ānanda, in space and on the earth who are earthly-minded; with dishevelled hair they weep, with uplifted arms they weep; flinging themselves on the ground, they roll from side to side, lamenting: 'Too soon has the Blessed One come to his Parinibbāna! Too soon has the Happy One come to his Parinibbāna! Too soon has the Eye of the World vanished from sight!' But those deities who are freed from passion, mindful and clearly comprehending, reflect in this way: 'Impermanent are all compounded things. How could this be otherwise?' "

19. Now the Venerable Anuruddha and the Venerable Ānanda spent the rest of the night in talking on the Dhamma. Then the Venerable Anuruddha spoke to the Venerable Ānanda, saying: "Go now, friend Ānanda, to Kusinārā, and announce to the Mallas: 'The Blessed One, Vāseṭṭhas, has passed away. Do now as seems fitting to you.' "

"So be it, venerable sir." And the Venerable Ānanda prepared himself in the forenoon, and taking bowl and robe, went with a companion into Kusinārā.

20. At that time the Mallas of Kusinārā had gathered in the council hall to consider that very matter. And the Venerable Ānanda approached them and announced: "The Blessed One, Vāseṭṭhas, has passed away. Do now as seems fitting to you."

And when they heard the Venerable Ānanda speak these words, the Mallas with their sons, their wives, and the wives of their sons, were sorely grieved, grieved at heart and afflicted; and some, with their hair all dishevelled, with arms upraised in despair, wept; flinging themselves on the ground, they rolled from side to side, lamenting: "Too soon has the Blessed One come to his Parinibbāna! "Too soon has the Happy One come to his Parinibbāna! Too soon has the Eye of the World vanished from sight!"

Homage to the Remains

21. Then the Mallas of Kusinārā gave orders to their men, saying: "Gather now all the perfumes, flower-garlands, and musicians, even all that are in Kusinārā." And the Mallas, with the perfumes, the flower-garlands, and the musicians, and with five hundred sets of clothing, went to the Sāla Grove, the recreation park of the Mallas, and approached the body of the Blessed One. And having approached, they paid homage to the body of the Blessed One with dance, song, music, flower-garlands, and perfume, and erecting canopies and pavilions, they spent the day showing respect, honour, and veneration to the body of the Blessed One. And then the thought came to them: "Now the day is too far spent for us to cremate the body of the Blessed One. Tomorrow we will do it."

And for the second day, and a third, fourth, fifth, and sixth day, they paid homage to the body of the Blessed One with dance, song, music, flower-garlands, and perfume, and erecting canopies and pavilions, they spent the day showing respect, honour, and veneration to the body of the Blessed One.

But on the seventh day the thought came to them: "We have paid homage to the body of the Blessed One with dance, song, music, flower-garlands, and perfume, and have shown respect, honour, and veneration; let us now carry the body of the Blessed One southward to the southern part of the town and beyond, and let us there cremate the body of the Blessed One south of the town."

And eight Mallas of the foremost families, bathed from the crown of their heads and wearing new clothes, with the thought: "We will lift up the body of the Blessed One," tried to do so but they could not.

22. Then the Mallas spoke to the Venerable Anuruddha, saying: "What is the cause, Venerable Anuruddha, what is the reason that these eight Mallas of the foremost families, bathed from the crown of their heads and wearing new clothes, with the thought: 'We will lift up the body of the Blessed One,' try to do so but cannot?"

"You, Vāseṭṭhas, have one purpose, the deities have another."

"Then what, venerable sir, is the purpose of the deities?"

"Your purpose, Vāseṭṭhas, is this: 'We have paid homage to the body of the Blessed One with dance, song, music, flower-garlands, and perfume, and have shown respect, honour, and veneration; let us now carry the body of the Blessed One southward to the southern part of the town and beyond, and let us there cremate the body of the Blessed One south of the town.' But the purpose of the deities, Vāseṭṭhas, is this: 'We have paid homage to the body of the Blessed One with heavenly dance, song, music, flower-garlands, and perfume, and have shown respect, honour, and veneration; let us now carry the body of the Blessed One northward to the northern part of the town; and having carried it through the northern gate, let us go through the centre of the town, and then eastward to the east of the town; and having passed through the east gate, let us carry it to the cetiya of the Mallas, Makuṭa-bandhana, and there let us cremate the body of the Blessed One.' "

"As the deities wish, venerable sir, so let it be."

23. Thereupon the whole of Kusinārā, even to the dust heaps and rubbish heaps, became covered knee-deep in *mandārava* flowers.[62] And homage was paid to the body of the Blessed One by the deities as well as the Mallas of Kusinārā. With dance, song, music, flower-garlands, and per-

fume, both divine and human, respect, honour, and veneration were shown. And they carried the body of the Blessed One northward to the northern part of the town; and having carried it through the northern gate, they went through the centre of the town, and then eastward to the east of the town; and having passed through the east gate, they carried the body of the Blessed One to the cetiya of the Mallas, Makuṭabandhana, and there laid it down.

24. Then the Mallas of Kusinārā spoke to the Venerable Ānanda, saying: "How should we act, Venerable Ānanda, respecting the body of the Tathāgata?"

"After the same manner, Vāseṭṭhas, as towards the body of a universal monarch."

"But how, venerable Ānanda, do they act respecting the body of a universal monarch?"

"The body of a universal monarch, Vāseṭṭhas, is first wrapped round with new linen, and then with teased cotton wool. And again it is wrapped round with new linen, and again with teased cotton wool, and so it is done up to five hundred layers of linen and five hundred of cotton wool. When that is done, the body of the universal monarch is placed in an iron oil-vessel, which is enclosed in another iron vessel and a funeral pyre is built of all kinds of perfumed woods, and so the body of the universal monarch is burned. And at a crossroads a stūpa is raised for the universal monarch. So it is done, Vāseṭṭhas, with the body of a universal monarch.

"And even, Vāseṭṭhas, as with the body of a universal monarch, so should it be done with the body of the Tathāgata; and at a crossroads also a stūpa should be raised for the Tathāgata. And whoever shall bring to that place garlands or incense or sandalwood paste, or pay reverence, and whose mind becomes calm there—it will be to his well being and happiness for a long time."

25. Then the Mallas gave orders to their men, saying: "Gather now all the teased cotton wool of the Mallas!" And the Mallas of Kusinārā wrapped the body of the Blessed One round with new linen, and then with teased cotton wool. And again they wrapped it round with new linen, and again with teased cotton wool, and so it was done up to five hundred layers of linen and five hundred of cotton wool. When that was done, they placed the body of the Blessed One in an iron oil-vessel, which was enclosed in another iron vessel, and they built a funeral pyre of all kinds of perfumed woods, and upon it they laid the body of the Blessed One.

26. Now at that time the Venerable Mahā Kassapa[63] was journeying from Pāvā to Kusinārā together with a large company of five hundred bhikkhus. And on the way, the Venerable Mahā Kassapa went aside from the highway and sat down at the foot of a tree.

And a certain Ājīvaka came by, on his way to Pāvā, and he had taken a *mandārava* flower from Kusinārā. And the Venerable Mahā Kassapa saw the Ājīvaka coming from a distance, and as he drew close he spoke to him, saying: "Do you know, friend, anything of our Master?"

"Yes, friend, I know. It is now seven days since the ascetic Gotama passed away. From there I have brought this *mandārava* flower."

27. Thereupon some bhikkhus, not yet freed from passion, lifted up their arms and wept; and some, flinging themselves on the ground, rolled from side to side and wept, lamenting: "Too soon has the Blessed One come to his Parinibbāna! Too soon has the Happy One come to his Parinibbāna! Too soon has the Eye of the World vanished from sight!"

28. Now at that time, one Subhadda, who had renounced only in his old age, was seated in the assembly.[64] And he addressed the bhikkhus, saying: "Enough, friends! Do not grieve, do not lament! We are well rid of that great ascetic. Too long, friends, have we been oppressed by his saying: 'This is fitting for you; that is not fitting for you.' Now we shall be able to do as we wish, and what we do not wish, that we shall not do."

But the Venerable Mahā Kassapa addressed the bhikkhus, saying: "Enough friends! Do not grieve, do not lament! For has not the Blessed One declared that with all that is dear and beloved there must be change, separation, and severance? Of that which is born, come into being, compounded, and subject to decay, how can one say: 'May it not come to dissolution!'?"

29. Now at that time four Mallas of the foremost families, bathed from the crown of their heads and wearing new clothes, with the thought: "We will set alight the Blessed One's pyre," tried to do so but they could not. And the Mallas spoke to the Venerable Anuruddha, saying: "What is the cause, Venerable Anuruddha, what is the reason that these four Mallas of the foremost families, bathed from the crown of their heads and wearing new clothes, with the thought: "We will set alight the Blessed One's pyre,' try to do so but cannot?"

"You, Vāseṭṭhas, have one purpose, the deities have another."

"Then what, venerable sir, is the purpose of the deities?"

"The purpose of the deities, Vāseṭṭhas, is this: 'The Venerable Mahā Kassapa is on his way from Pāvā to Kusinārā together with a large company of five hundred bhikkhus. Let not the Blessed One's pyre be set alight until the Venerable

Mahā Kassapa has paid homage at the feet of the Blessed One.' "

"As the deities wish, venerable sir, so let it be."

30. And the Venerable Mahā Kassapa approached the pyre of the Blessed One, at the cetiya of the Mallas, Makuṭa-bandhana, in Kusinārā. And he arranged his upper robe on one shoulder, and with his clasped hands raised in salutation, he walked three times round the pyre, keeping his right side towards the Blessed One's body, and he paid homage at the feet of the Blessed One. And even so did the five hundred bhikkhus.

And when homage had been paid by the Venerable Mahā Kassapa and the five hundred bhikkhus, the pyre of the Blessed One burst into flame by itself.

31. And it came about that when the body of the Blessed One had been burned, no ashes or particles were to be seen of what had been skin, tissue, flesh, sinews, and fluid; only bones remained. Just as when ghee or oil is burned, it leaves no particles or ashes behind, even so when the body of the Blessed One had been burned, no ashes or particles were to be seen of what had been skin, tissue, flesh, sinews, and fluid; only bones remained. And of the five hundred linen wrappings, only two were not consumed, the innermost and the outermost.

32. And when the body of the Blessed One had been burned, water rained down from heaven and extinguished the pyre of the Blessed One, and from the sāla trees water came forth, and the Mallas of Kusinārā brought water scented with many kinds of perfumes, and they too extinguished the pyre of the Blessed One.

And the Mallas of Kusinārā laid the relics of the Blessed One in their council hall, and surrounded them with a lattice-work of spears and encircled them with a fence of bows;

and there for seven days they paid homage to the relics of the Blessed One with dance, song, music, flower-garlands, and perfume, and showed respect, honour, and veneration to the relics of the Blessed One.

Partition of the Relics

33. Then the king of Magadha, Ajātasattu, son of the Videhi queen, came to know that at Kusinārā the Blessed One had passed away. And he sent a message to the Mallas of Kusinārā, saying: "The Blessed One was of the warrior caste, and I am too. I am worthy to receive a portion of the relics of the Blessed One. I will erect a stūpa over the relics of the Blessed One and hold a festival in their honour."

34. And the Licchavis of Vesālī came to know that at Kusinārā the Blessed One had passed away. And they sent a message to the Mallas of Kusinārā, saying: "The Blessed One was of the warrior caste, and we are too. We are worthy to receive a portion of the relics of the Blessed One. We will erect a stūpa over the relics of the Blessed One and hold a festival in their honour."

35. And the Sakyas of Kapilavatthu came to know that at Kusinārā the Blessed One had passed away. And they sent a message to the Mallas of Kusinārā, saying: "The Blessed One was the greatest of our clan. We are worthy to receive a portion of the relics of the Blessed One. We will erect a stūpa over the relics of the Blessed One and hold a festival in their honour."

36. And the Bulis of Allakappa came to know that at Kusinārā the Blessed One had passed away. And they sent a message to the Mallas of Kusinārā, saying: "The Blessed One was of the warrior caste, and we are too. We are worthy to receive a portion of the relics of the Blessed One. We will

erect a stūpa over the relics of the Blessed One and hold a festival in their honour."

37. And the Kolis of Rāmagāma came to know that at Kusinārā the Blessed One had passed away. And they sent a message to the Mallas of Kusinārā, saying: "The Blessed One was of the warrior caste, and we are too. We are worthy to receive a portion of the relics of the Blessed One. We will erect a stūpa over the relics of the Blessed One and hold a festival in their honour."

38. And the Veṭhadīpa brahmin came to know that at Kusinārā the Blessed One had passed away. And he sent a message to the Mallas of Kusinārā, saying: "The Blessed One was of the warrior caste, and I am a brahmin. I am worthy to receive a portion of the relics of the Blessed One. I will erect a stūpa over the relics of the Blessed One and hold a festival in their honour."

39. And the Mallas of Pāvā came to know that at Kusinārā the Blessed One had passed away. And they sent a message to the Mallas of Kusinārā, saying: "The Blessed One was of the warrior caste, and we are too. We are worthy to receive a portion of the relics of the Blessed One. We will erect a stūpa over the relics of the Blessed One and hold a festival in their honour."

40. But when they heard these words, the Mallas of Kusinārā addressed the assembly, saying: "The Blessed One has passed away in our township. We shall not part with any portion of the relics of the Blessed One." Then the brahmin Doṇa spoke to the assembly, saying:

> "One word from me, I beg you, sirs, to hear!
> Our Buddha taught us ever to forbear;
> Unseemly would it be should strife arise
> And war and bloodshed, over the custody
> Of his remains, who was the best of men!

Let us all, sirs, in friendliness agree
To share eight portions—so that far and wide
Stūpas may rise, and seeing them, mankind
Faith in the All-Enlightened One will find!"

"So be it, brahmin! Divide the relics into eight equal portions yourself."

And the brahmin Doṇa said to the assembly: "So be it, sirs." And he divided justly into eight equal portions the relics of the Blessed One, and having done so, he addressed the assembly, saying: "Let this urn, sirs, be given to me. Over this urn I will erect a stūpa, and in its honour I will hold a festival." And the urn was given to the brahmin Doṇa.

41. Then the Moriyas of Pipphalivana came to know that at Kusinārā the Blessed One had passed away. And they sent a message to the Mallas of Kusinārā, saying: "The Blessed One was of the warrior caste, and we are too. We are worthy to receive a portion of the relics of the Blessed One. We will erect a stūpa over the relics of the Blessed One and hold a festival in their honour."

"There is no portion of the relics of the Blessed One remaining; the relics of the Blessed One have been divided. But take from here the ashes." And they took from there the ashes.

42. And the king of Magadha, Ajātasattu, son of the Videhi queen, erected a stūpa over the relics of the Blessed One at Rājagaha, and in their honour held a festival. The Licchavis of Vesālī erected a stūpa over the relics of the Blessed One at Vesālī, and in their honour held a festival. The Sakyas of Kapilavatthu erected a stūpa over the relics of the Blessed One at Kapilavatthu, and in their honour held a festival. The Bulis of Allakappa erected a stūpa over the relics of the Blessed One at Allakappa, and in their honour held a festival. The Kolis of Rāmagāma erected a stūpa over the relics

of the Blessed One at Rāmagāma, and in their honour held a festival. The Veṭhadīpa brahmin erected a stūpa over the the relics of the Blessed One at Veṭhadīpa, and in their honour held a festival. The Mallas of Pāvā erected a stūpa over the relics of the Blessed One at Pāvā, and in their honour held a festival. The Mallas of Kusinārā erected a stūpa over the relics of the Blessed One at Kusinārā, and in their honour held a festival. The brahmin Doṇa erected a stūpa over the urn, and in its honour held a festival. And the Moriyas of Pipphalivana erected a stūpa over the ashes at Pipphalivana, and in their honour held a festival.

So it came about that there were eight stūpas for the relics, a ninth for the urn, and a tenth for the ashes.

And thus it was in the days of old.

43. Eight portions there were of the relics of him,
The All-Seeing One, the greatest of men.
Seven in Jambudipa are honoured, and one
In Rāmagāma, by kings of the Nāga race.
One tooth is honoured in the Tāvatiṁsa heaven,
One in the realm of Kaliṅga, and one by the Nāga kings.
Through their brightness this bountiful earth
With its most excellent gifts is endowed;
For thus the relics of the All-Seeing One are best honoured
By those who are worthy of honour—by gods and Nāgas
And lords of men, yea, by the highest of mankind.
Pay homage with clasped hands! For hard indeed it is
Through hundreds of ages to meet with an All-Enlightened One![65]

The Mahāparinibbāna Sutta is ended.

Notes

[References to Anguttara Nikāya (= AN) are to collection followed by sutta number; those to Dīgha Nikāya (= DN) and to Majjhima Nikāya (= MN) are to sutta number.]

1. *Bhagavā*: also rendered "the Auspicious One" or "the Exalted One"; the most frequent appellation of the Buddha, though not restricted to Buddhist usage.
2. *Ajātasattu Vedehiputta*. Comy. says that Ajātasattu's mother was a Kosala princess and not the daughter of the Vedehi king. Hence Comy. explains *vedehiputta* as "son of a wise mother." Ajātasattu became king of the powerful state of Magadha after murdering his father, King Bimbisāra (see DN 2).
3. *Tathāgata*: lit. "Thus-gone" or "Thus-come"; likewise an appellation of the Buddha, which he generally used when speaking of himself.
4. Ānanda was a cousin of the Buddha and his personal attendant for twenty-four years. He attained arahatship after the passing away of the Buddha, just before the commencement of the First Council, at which he was the reciter of the Dīgha Nikāya and the authority for the Sutta Piṭaka.
5. The discourse referred to here is AN 7:19.
6. The group-names, which are not in the original, are supplied from other references to the qualities concerned; here *satta saddhammā*, about which see AN 7:63; MN 53. In the Comy. to MN 8 they are called "the complete equipment required for insight" (BPS Wheel No. 61/62, p.48).
7. *Satta bojjhaṅgā*. See Piyadassi Thera, *The Seven Factors of Enlightenment* (BPS Wheel No. 1).

8. *Sāraṇiyā dhammā*: also at MN 48, AN 6:11, 12.
9. Virtue (*sīla*), concentration (*samādhi*), and wisdom (*paññā*) are the three divisions of the Noble Eightfold Path. Our text stresses again and again the importance of a full development of all three for final liberation.
10. *Āsava*: those defiling factors—sensual desire, craving for existence, and ignorance—primarily responsible for maintaining bondage to the cycle of rebirths. Also translated as "cankers" or "corruptions." Later texts add a fourth, the taint of wrong views.
11. Sāriputta was the chief disciple of the Buddha and the one who excelled in wisdom. For a full account of his life and works, see Nyanaponika Thera, *The Life of Sāriputta* (BPS Wheel No. 90/92).
12. *Evaṁ-dhammā*. Comy. & Sub. Comy.: This refers to concentration and to the mental qualities belonging to concentration (*samādhipakkhiyā dhammā*) such as energy, mindfulness, etc. Comy. explains "abiding" (*vihāra*) as abiding in the attainment of cessation (*nirodha-samāpatti*).
13. *Evaṁ-vimuttā*: their deliverance from defilements and from future rebirths.
14. On the five hindrances, see Nyanaponika Thera, *The Five Mental Hindrances* (BPS Wheel No. 26).
15. On the four foundations of mindfulness, see below, II:14. The seven factors of enlightenment are enumerated in I:9.
16. *Puṭa-bhedanaṁ*. Comy. explains as the breaking open, the unpacking, of boxes (*puṭa*) of merchandise for the purpose of distribution. But probably it refers to the bursting open of the seed-box of the *pāṭali* flower.
17. The stage of arahatship, the last of the four stages of deliverance. The next three paragraphs refer to disciples on the three lower stages, respectively, the non-returner, once-returner, and stream-enterer (*anāgāmi, sakadāgāmi, sotāpanna*).
18. Or: "not delayed (in its results)."

19. *Animitta cetosamādhi*. Comy. explains this term here as referring to the fruition-attainment of arahatship (*phalasamāpatti*), in which the Buddha becomes absorbed in the direct experience of Nibbāna and no longer attends to external objects or feels mundane feelings. In another context it can mean the concentration developed by intensive insight.

20. *Tamatagge*: a difficult word. Comy. takes it to stand for the superlative form, *aggatamā*, "highest," but alludes also to the Pāli word *tama*, "darkness." It is rather difficult to accept that a superlative suffix should be made to precede the word it qualifies. Tibetan and Chinese parallels (Waldschmidt, *Das Mahāparinirvāṇa-sūtra* Berlin, 1950–51) pp. 200 ff.) point to a meaning as "the highest." In the fragments of the Turfan Sanskrit version, these words are not preserved. Comy. says: "*Tamatagge* = *tama-agge*; the 't' in the middle is inserted for euphonic reasons. The meaning is: these are the very highest, the most eminent (*ime aggatamā tamataggā*). Having cut every bondage of darkness (*tama-yoga*), those bhikkhus of mine will be on the very top, in the highest rank (*ativiya agge uttamabhāve*). Among them those will be on the very summit (*ati-agge*) who are desirous of training; and those whose resort is the four foundations of mindfulness will be at the very top of them."

21. *Kappaṁ vā tiṭṭheyya kappāvasesaṁ vā*. Comy. takes *kappa* not as "world-period" or "aeon," but as *āyu-kappa*, "life span," and explains *avasesa* (usually "remainder") by "in excess."

Comy.: "He may stay alive completing the life span pertaining to men at the given time. (Sub. Comy.: the maximum life span.) *Kappāvasesa*: 'in excess' (*atireka*), i.e. more or less above the hundred years said to be the normally highest life expectation."

Among the numerous meanings of the word *kappa*, there is, in fact, that of time in general (*kāla*) and not only the duration of an aeon; but the meaning "life span" seems to have been ascribed to it only in this passage. Also, the meaning "in excess" for *avasesa* (usually "remainder") is unusual.

The four constituents of psychic power (*iddhipāda*) are concentration due to zeal, energy, purity of mind, and investigation.

22. According to Comy., Ānanda's mind had been influenced (*pariyuṭṭhitacitto*) by Māra's exhibiting a frightful sight which distracted his attention, preventing him from grasping the Buddha's suggestion.

23. "Convincing and liberating." This stands for the one Pāli word *sappāṭihāriya*, an attempt to render the two connotations which the word has according to the commentaries and in the context of other occurrences in the Canon. The commentaries derive it from the verb *paṭiharati*, "to remove," and explain it as (1) the removal of what is adverse, e.g. opposition and objections (covered by "convincing"), and (2) the removal of inner obstructions, i.e. defilements such as greed, etc., effected by arahatship. It is probably to point to that latter meaning that the commentary to our present text paraphrases our passage as follows: "until they are able to preach the Teaching in its liberating (*niyyānika*) capacity."

24. *Tulaṁ atulañca sambhavaṁ*: lit. "the measurable and immeasurable productive cause (of life)," i.e. the volitional action causing rebirth in the confined, or limited sense-sphere, or in the unbounded fine-material and immaterial spheres.

25. *Bhavasaṅkhāra*: the formative force of becoming, in the sense of what forms existence.

26. *Kavacam iv'attasambhavaṁ*. Comy.: "He breaks through the entire net of defilements that envelops individual existence like a coat of mail; he breaks the defilements as a great warrior breaks his armour after a battle." The Sanskrit version has "like an egg shell" (*kosam iv' aṇḍa-sambhavaṁ*).

27. Comy.: "Even by this much the Venerable Ānanda was aware of the fact: 'Surely, today the Blessed One has renounced his will to live on.' Though the Blessed One knew that the Venerable Ānanda was aware of it, he did not give him another opportunity to ask him to stay on for the remainder of his life span, but he spoke to him about other eight-term groups beginning with the eight assemblies." Sub. Comy.:

"Some say that the Buddha did so in order to divert the Venerable Ānanda and to prevent grief from arising in him."

28. See also the Mahāsīhanāda Sutta (MN 12).

29. *Abhibhāyatana.*

30. That is: "perceiving forms on his own body." This refers to preliminary concentration.

31. This refers to the *kasiṇa-nimitta*, the after-image arising with full concentration.

32. He derives the "sign" from objects external to his body.

33. *Aṭṭha vimokkhā.*

34. *Rūpī.* This refers to form-sphere absorption (*rūpajjhāna*) obtained with form objects of one's own body.

35. *Subhan tveva adhimutto hoti.* Comy.: "Hereby, meditative absorption (*jhāna*), obtained through *blue-kasiṇas*, etc., of very pure colour is indicated."

36. The Comy. says that the Buddhas, when looking back, turn the whole body round as an elephant does.

37. In the earlier edition of this work, *mahāpadesa* was rendered as "great authorities." It is now known that the proper meaning of *apadesa* is not "authority," but "reference" or "source." Besides, from the passage it is clear that there are only two real "authorities"—the Discourses (Suttas) and the Discipline (Vinaya).

38. *Sūkara-maddava*: a controversial term which has therefore been left untranslated. *Sūkara* = pig; *maddava* = soft, tender, delicate. Hence two alternative renderings of the compound are possible: (1) the tender parts *of* a pig or boar; (2) what is enjoyed *by* pigs and boars. In the latter meaning, the term has been thought to refer to a mushroom or truffle, or a yam or tuber. K.E. Neumann, in the preface to his German translation of the Majjhima Nikāya, quotes from an Indian compendium of medicinal plants, the *Rājanigaṇṭu*, several plants beginning with *sūkara*.

The commentary to our text gives three alternative explanations: (1) the flesh from a single first-born (wild) pig, neither too young nor too old, which had come to hand naturally, i.e. without intentional killing; (2) a preparation of soft boiled rice cooked with the five cow-products; (3) a kind of alchemistic elixir (*rasāyanavidhi*). Dhammapāla, in his commentary to Udāna 8:5, gives, in addition, young bamboo shoots trampled by pigs (*sūkarehi maddita-vaṁsakalīro*).

39. Comy.: "These verses, and several to follow, were inserted by the elders who collected the Dhamma (texts at the First Council)."

40. Āḷāra Kālāma was one of the Buddha's teachers before his Enlightenment. He taught the Bodhisatta how to attain the sphere of nothingness, but could not show him the path to Nibbāna.

41. Comy.: "From the town of Pāvā it is three *gāvutas* (approx. five miles) to Kusinārā. Walking that distance with great effort and sitting down at twenty-five places on the way, the Blessed One reached the Sāla Grove at dusk when the sun had already set. Thus comes illness to man, crushing all his health. As if he wanted to point to this fact, the Blessed One spoke those words which deeply moved the whole world: 'I am weary, Ānanda, and want to lie down.' "

42. See *The Four Sacred Shrines*, by Piyadassi Thera (BPS Bodhi Leaves No. 8).

43. At Lumbini near Kapilavatthu, the ancestral seat of the Sakyans in the foothills of the Himalayas. An Asokan pillar marks the spot.

44. At Buddha-Gayā, in Bihar.

45. At Isipatana near Benares (modern Sarnath).

46. *Sadatthe*. Comy.: "for the highest purpose, the goal of arahatship." There is a different reading, *sāratthe*, "for an essential purpose."

47. *Cakkavatti-rājā*: the ideal king of righteousness according to Buddhist tradition.

48. *Āyasa*: generally "made of iron," has here according to Comy. the meaning "made of gold," for which there is also support in the Sanskrit usage of the word.

49. *Paccekabuddha* is one awakened or enlightened for himself alone. Such Paccekabuddhas arise at times when there is no Fully Enlightened One (*sammā-sambuddha*). Like the latter, they attain to Enlightenment by their own effort, but unlike them are not able to lead others to deliverance. See Ria Kloppenberg, *The Paccekabuddha: A Buddhist Ascetic* (BPS Wheel No. 305/307).

50. The word *vihāra*, given in the text, cannot refer here to a monastery or monks' living quarters. Comy. explains it as a pavilion (*maṇḍala-māla*). If the locality was used as a meeting place for the clan, as Comy. states, there may well have been a kind of shelter there. The couch in the open, which Ānanda was asked to prepare for the Master, was probably a seat for the chiefs of the Malla clan put up at that place.

51. *Sekha*. This signifies those at the three lower stages of emanicipation, before reaching arahatship. Ānanda, at that time, had reached the first of these stages, stream-entry.

52. *Anāsavo*: that is, an arahat.

53. The "seven jewels" of a universal monarch are: the magical wheel, emblem of his sovereignty, by which he conquers the earth without the use of force; his wonderful elephant; his horse; his beautiful wife; his precious gem; his treasurer; and his advisor. All are endowed with wondrous properties. For more on Mahā Sudassana, see the sutta which bears his name, DN 17.

54. The four degrees of saintliness are the stream-enterer, the once-returner, the non-returner, and the arahat.

55. "Friend," in Pali is *āvuso*, "venerable sir" = *bhante*, "your reverence" = *āyasmā*.

56. Since Ānanda, at this point, did not ask what the minor rules were, the Sangha decided not to abolish any of the rules of the Vinaya.

57. Channa had been the Buddha's charioteer while the latter was still a prince living in the palace. Because of his prior connection with the Buddha, he was obdurate and refused

to submit to discipline. This imposition of the "higher penalty" (*brahmadaṇḍa*) changed him into an obedient monk.

58. *Handa dāni bhikkhave āmantayāmi vo: Vayadhammā saṅkhārā appamādena sampādetha.* Earnestness (*appamāda*) is explained as "presence of mindfulness." Comy.: "'You should accomplish all your duties without allowing mindfulness to lapse!' Thus did the Blessed One, while on the bed of his Parinibbāna, summarize in that one word on earnestness the advice he had given through forty-five years."

59. Anuruddha, the elder brother of Ānanda, would have known this through the super-normal power of reading the minds of others, which he possessed.

60. Brahmā Sahampati was a high divinity of the Brahma-world. It was he who originally requested the newly enlightened Buddha to teach the Dhamma to the world. See MN 26.

61. Sakka is the king of the gods in the Tāvatiṁsa heaven, and thus a lower figure in the cosmological hierarchy than Brahmā Sahampati.

62. A celestial flower which appears on earth only on special occasions, particularly in connection with the chief events in the life of the Buddha. Its appearance in the hands of the Ājīvaka ascetic signalled to the Venerable Mahā Kassapa that the Buddha's Parinibbāna had already taken place. (See below, Section 26.)

63. He was one of the foremost disciples of the Buddha and became the president of the First Great Council held shortly after the Buddha's Parinibbāna. See Helmuth Hecker, *Mahā Kassapa: Father of the Sangha* (BPS Wheel No. 345).

64. This Subhadda is a different person from the wanderer Subhadda who became the Buddha's last personal disciple.

65. Comy. ascribes these verses to the "Elders of Tambapaṇṇi Island (Sri Lanka)."

Available from BPS

THE LIFE OF THE BUDDHA
According to the Pāli Canon

Bhikkhu Ñāṇamoli

Numerous lives of the Buddha have been written and translated, but this volume, with its comprehensive material and original method of presentation, may well claim a place of its own. Composed entirely from texts of the Pāli Canon, the oldest authentic record, it portrays an image of the Buddha—the great Master of Wisdom and Compassion—which is vivid, warm, and moving. The ancient texts are rendered in a language marked by lucidity and dignity as befits the beauty of the original. They are presented in a framework of "narrators" and "voices" which serves to connect the canonical texts through historical notes and other informations thus giving coherence to the narrative. The book also includes a chapter on the Buddha's doctrine that is highly illuminating and has a distinct flavour of its own. This is a book that can inform and inspire.

THE BUDDHIST PUBLICATION SOCIETY

The BPS is an approved charity dedicated to making known the Teaching of the Buddha, which has a vital message for people of all creeds. Founded in 1958, the BPS has published a wide variety of books and booklets covering a great range of topics. Its publications include accurate annotated translations of the Buddha's discourses, standard reference works, as well as original contemporary expositions of Buddhist thought and practice. These works present Buddhism as it truly is—a dynamic force which has influenced receptive minds for the past 2500 years and is still as relevant today as it was when it first arose. A full list of our publications will be sent upon request. Write to:

The Hony. Secretary
BUDDHIST PUBLICATION SOCIETY
P.O. Box 61
54, Sangharaja Mawatha
Kandy • Sri Lanka
E–mail: bps@mail.lanka.net
Website: http: //www.lanka.com/dhamma